MARK ALLEN BERRYHILL

WESTBOW
PRESS®
A DIVISION OF THOMAS NELSON
& ZONDERVAN

Scripture taken from the King James Version of the Bible.

WestBow Press books may be ordered through booksellers or by contacting:

WestBow Press
A Division of Thomas Nelson & Zondervan
1663 Liberty Drive
Bloomington, IN 47403
www.westbowpress.com
1 (866) 928-1240

ISBN: 978-1-9736-3738-7 (sc)
ISBN: 978-1-9736-3739-4 (hc)
ISBN: 978-1-9736-3737-0 (e)

Library of Congress Control Number: 2018909825

Print information available on the last page.

WestBow Press rev. date: 08/20/2018

God the Father, the Lord Jesus Christ and the Holy Spirit

By Mark Berryhill

Table of Contents

The Importance of Daily Prayer and Daily Bible Study

The importance of daily prayer and Bible study can equate to the difference between eternal salvation and eternal separation from God. Without God in our continual thoughts and daily lives, our hearts become hardened by the cares of this world and by the deceitfulness of riches.

> And he spake many things unto them in parables, saying, Behold, a sower went forth to sow; And when he sowed, some seeds fell by the way side, and the fowls came and devoured them up: Some fell upon stony places, where they had not much earth: and forthwith they sprung up, because they had no deepness of the earth: And when the sun was up, they were scorched; and because they had no root, they withered away. And some fell among thorns; and the thorns sprung up, and choked them: But other fell into good ground, and brought forth fruit, some a hundredfold, some sixty-fold, some thirty. Who hath ears to hear, let them hear.[1]

As Solomon wrote in Proverbs, "Keep thy heart with all diligence; for out of it are the issues of life."[2] God molds and softens our hearts as we pray and study His Word on a daily basis.

Father, thank You for the wonderful parents You blessed me with. Thank You for a mother who had me in church worshipping You while I was young and tender. Thank You for a father who stood by me and was there for me when many fathers would have deserted their sons.

---

[1] Matthew 13:3–9.
[2] Proverbs 4:23.

God says that if we draw near to Him, He will draw near to us. I want God to be not only my Father but the Father of each one of us. Father, thank You for Your Son and my Savior, the Lord Jesus Christ. Please help me and those who read this book to keep in mind at all times the importance of repentance and baptism in the name of Jesus Christ for the remission of sins and the importance of walking daily in the light. Give us the strength, discipline, and fortitude we need to keep ourselves holy, blameless, and spotless until the appearance of our Lord Jesus Christ.

Father, teach us to live in the Spirit and not in the uncleanness of the flesh. Father, teach us and train us to be godly. Father, pardon me of the sins I committed against You in the past. I pray that You will give us Your Holy Spirit without measure so that we will walk in the light and please You. Father, thank You for the blood of the Lamb that continually cleanses us from all sin provided we walk in the light.

Father, I pray for Your divine intervention, not only for us here in the United States of America, but also for the people of all the nations of the world.

Lord Jesus, thank You for sacrificing Your life for us. Help us to never take for granted the grace, mercy, and truth that You and God the Father have extended to each of us who diligently seek You and obey Your commandments. Help us to never sin willfully, knowing that "For if we sin willfully after that we have received the knowledge of the truth, there remaineth no more sacrifice for sins, But a certain fearful looking for of judgment and fiery indignation, which shall devour the adversaries."[3]

Father, give us the wisdom and knowledge to meditate on Your Word on a daily basis, realizing that Your Word is a lamp for our feet in a world full of wickedness. Elohim, before the foundation of the world, You prepared an eternal home in the heavens for those who love You and obey the gospel of our Lord Jesus Christ. Father, teach me to love You with all of my heart, soul, mind, and strength. Even if You slay me, Lord, I will trust in You.

Lord God, I pray You will teach Your precious children Your Word each day. Where are You, Father? There is so much work that

---

[3] Hebrews 10:26–27.

must be done. We need Your love. We need You to be our God. Father, remember Your servant Abraham and Your covenant with him, Isaac, and Jacob. Write Your Word on our hearts and in our minds, almighty Father.

Teach us Your precepts. Bless us with all wisdom, knowledge, understanding, and revelation concerning Your will. Lead us in the pathways of righteousness and holiness for Your great name's sake.

I pray, Father, You will give Your friends the courage to proclaim Your Word boldly, knowing it is Your power unto eternal salvation. Bless us with the Spirit of wisdom and love, Lord God! Love us and mold us with Your skillful hands, Lord Jesus. Lord Jesus, You are the Great Shepherd and bishop of our souls. Lead us in righteousness, Lord Jesus.

Thank You for today, Lord Jesus. Thank You for Your Word, Most High. Father, help us to pursue kindness, gentleness, and humility at all times. Help me to never be arrogant or haughty or to consider myself wise in mine own eyes or conceit. Lord God, "Remove far from me vanity and lies; give me neither poverty nor riches; feed me with food convenient for me."[4]

Thank You, Father, for our children, who bring such joy, happiness, and goodness into our lives. Help us to be perfect examples before them in all godliness, holiness, and righteousness. Father, love our children and mold them with Your skillful hands. Write Your Word in their hearts and minds. Place within their hearts and minds hunger and thirst for righteousness. Lord Jesus, You are our strength, our refuge, and our great reward. Protect us, love us, and guide us in the pathway of truth, Lord Jesus.

Thank You for forgiving me of my past sins, Lord God. Thank You for Jesus and His blood, which washes me from all sin and enables me to come boldly to the throne of grace.

Father, make us holy men and holy women. Help those who are unmarried to be pure and holy in the flesh and in the Spirit, knowing that the fervent prayers of the righteous avail much.

Father, we need You near us. We need You to be our Father, and we need Your guidance and direction in our daily lives. I love You, Lord Jesus. I love You, Lord God. I love You, Holy Spirit.

---

[4] Proverbs 30:8.

I am weak, Lord Jesus, but You are strong. I am a sinner, yet You are holy. Thank You for being holy, Lord God. Thank You for loving me, and thank You for discipling me.

I love Your Word, Lord God. Thank You for Your great Word, Lord God. Thank You for the purity and holiness Your Word brings into our lives. As Your servant David, help us to meditate on Your Word day and night. Make us to know that our lives are but a vapor, a mist, and a shadow when compared to eternal life with You or eternal separation from You. Thank You for Your Word and for Your Son and our Savior Jesus.

Help us to be accounted worthy to stand before Jesus on the great and notable day of the Lord and accounted worthy of eternal life with You. Your great Word says we will be judged by our words and works. For by our words we will be justified, and by our words we will be condemned. Teach us to be quick to listen, slow to speak, and slow to wrath. "For by thy words thou shalt be justified, and by thy words thou shalt be condemned."[5] The Word also states, "For as the body without the spirit is dead, so faith without works is dead also."[6] "And, behold, I come quickly; and my reward is with me, to give every man according as his work shall be."[7]

May we always extend love and help those who are in need. Your Word says that by having helped those in need unbeknownst to them, they may have entertained angels. Father, make us holy men and holy women. Thank You for having called us out of the darkness and into Your marvelous light.

In the name of the
Father, the Son, and
the Holy Ghost,

Amen and Amen.

---

[5] Matthew 12:37.
[6] James 2:26.
[7] Revelation 22:12.

Abortion Is Wrong

Abortion is wrong. Please read Exodus 20:13, Mark 3:4, Luke 6:9, and Galatians 5:19–21. There is a solution to abortion. According to God's Word, neither fornicators nor murderers will inherit the kingdom of God. When people have sexual intercourse without being married to each other, it is in direct contradiction to the Word of God. It is absolutely true that the precious babies who are aborted are protected by the angels of God and will spend eternity with God. Where will the parents who allow their children to be aborted, the doctors who perform the abortions, and the lawmakers who have allowed abortion to continue in this country spend eternity? If the righteous will scarcely be saved, what about the ungodly?

How can we expect our children to walk in the light when we have not adequately explained to them the eternal reward for those who love the Lord and are obedient to His commandments? We must explain the eternal penalty for those who do not love God and are disobedient to the commandments of the Lord. Forgive us of the sins of youth, almighty Father.

In the name of the
Father, the Son, and
the Holy Ghost,

Amen and Amen.

Invisible, Visible, Invisible

The following is made law and placed into effect immediately in the United States of America and throughout the world.

1. The production and distribution of pornography is made illegal in this nation and throughout the world.
2. All bars are to be closed and made illegal in this nation and throughout the world.
3. Prostitution is made illegal in this nation and throughout the world.
4. Drug trafficking is made illegal in this nation and throughout the world.
5. The production of all intoxicating liquors is made illegal in this nation and throughout the world.
6. The production of all books, writings, movies, and so on that do not glorify the Lord are made illegal in this nation and throughout the world.
7. All businesses are to be closed on Saturday to honor the Lord of Sabbath.

In the name of the
Father, the Son and
the Holy Ghost

Amen and Amen
Copyright © 2008

Extending Mercy

A prayer by Mark Berryhill

Capital punishment is wrong. Please read Exodus 20:13, Matthew 6:14, 15 and Luke 6:9.

When a person has committed a murder or murders, he or she should spend the remainder of life in prison. Capital punishment is wrong. God says that we are not to kill and that we are to forgive each other of our trespasses.

If a person has committed a murder and has sincerely repented of the sin, confessed that Jesus Christ is the Son of God, and been baptized for the remission of sins, that person should be extended mercy and compassion. If we extend mercy to others, God says that He will extend mercy to us. There is, and always have been, consequences for sin. Death is the consequence of man's sin in the garden. Each of us return to dust soon enough.

In the name of the
Father, the Son and
the Holy Ghost

Amen and Amen
Copyright © 2008

Worshipping in Spirit and in Truth

A prayer by Mark Berryhill

The greatest pleasure and fulfillment in life is to sit down and diligently study the Word of God. As we study the life of Jesus and the words that He spoke while He was on the earth, we discover very quickly that He spent the majority of His time studying God's Word before He actually began teaching and preaching the kingdom of Heaven on a daily basis. Jesus always backed His responses with Scripture.

In order for us to be able to respond to questions about God and His Word, we must be knowledgeable in the Word of God ourselves. How can we teach our children the Word of God if we do not know the Word of God?

As we begin to study God's Word on a daily basis, we discover the Lord strengthening us very rapidly. God is Spirit and wants to be worshipped in Spirit and in truth.

Two ways we acknowledge our love for the Lord is to diligently study His Word on a daily basis and to pray to Him not only on a daily basis, but without ceasing. Jesus says that if we love Him, we will keep His commandments.

The second greatest pleasure in life is spending time with children whom the Lord has so graciously loaned to us for the short length of time we spend on the earth.

At this time, my son Nathan is six years old and my daughter Evan is four years old. Recently, while Nathan, Evan and I were at Lake Amistad, which is just outside of Del Rio, Texas, I noticed how loving and caring both Nathan and Evan are. Nathan is extremely protective of his younger sister.

As all young children, they have disagreements but, in general, they get along with each other extremely well.

Back to the lake trip. I had bought Nathan and Evan some small boats to play with in the lake. While Nathan was pushing one of the boats in the water, God caused a whirlwind to blow where we were playing. Nathan's response to the whirlwind, which was caused by God, was adorable. Nathan tilted his head toward Heaven and responded to the Lord, "Hey, we're playing down here."

Have you ever considered how much fun God and Jesus have playing with and taking care of their children. God is all knowing, all powerful and yet desires to be our full time Father and friend. Many of us have misunderstood the relationship God desires to have with each one of us. He wants us to be in communion with Him as were His servants of old.

In the name of the
Father, the Son and
the Holy Ghost

Amen and Amen
Copyright © 2008

The Beginning of Prayers

A prayer by Mark Berryhill

Father, we long to be with You. We long for the eternal security that only You can provide.

We desire love and not hate. We desire peace and friendship, not war. We desire for You to be our Father, our Lord, our God, and our King.

We want not only the temporal protection You provide for us, but also the eternal protection You have promised to those who love You, and obey Your commandments.

I pray for Your divine intervention into the lives and affairs of the people throughout the world.

Be our God, for we are Your people. We seek purity, righteousness and holiness. We pursue love, mercy, kindness and compassion.

Father, teach us to love You and to trust You with all of our hearts, with all of our souls, with all of our minds and with all of our strength.

Bless us with the fruit of Your Spirit: bless us with love, joy, peace, longsuffering, gentleness, goodness, faith, meekness and temperance.

Bless us with love and wisdom. Teach us to walk and to live in the Spirit.

In the name of the
Father, the Son and
the Holy Ghost

Amen and Amen
Copyright © 2008

A Prayer of Trust

A prayer by Mark Berryhill

Father, teach us to love You with total abandonment of ourselves. May I trust in You, even if You slay me, knowing that my name is written in the Lamb's book of life.

May our eyes be ever fixed on our Lord Jesus, and our minds dwelling on the eternal, and not on the temporal.

As the rain from Heaven, so is Your faithfulness to me, my Lord, my God and my King.

As the dew gently settles on the golden pastures, so is the purity and holiness of the great King.

As the fruit of the womb, so is the gift of our God's Christ. The King, the Christ, He alone is my all in all. He and He alone is provision.

In the night visions and in the night watches, my Lord resides with me. Yes, and in the valley of the shadow of death, my God sustained me.

I will not fear what man may do unto me, my Lord is the avenger.

My Lord, my God, my King! Tell me Holy One, how far is the east from the west, or how far is the north from the south?

Where was I my Lord when You bound the Orion, the Pleiades, and the Arctures?

Great, how great is Your faithfulness! King of Israel, how great is Your enduring love!

In laughter You are with me, and in sadness You are with me.

You are my strength, my fortress, my shield, my rock and my redeemer. I will hope in You, yes, I will trust in You.

At sunrise You will hear my prayer. At noontime You will hear my prayer. Without ceasing I will pray unto my Lord.

God is a God of comfort and a God of strength.

Fill us with the purity and holiness only Your Word can bring into our daily lives.

In dreams and visions of the night, the Lord is with me.

The Christ, the Messiah, the Holy One of God is our hope, our love and our light.

As the newborn baby cries for her mother, so will we fret about our King.

As the newborn fawn needs her mother's milk, so will we crave our Father's eternal provision.

A God of war is my God. A God of peace is our King. Holy, Holy, Holy Lord God Almighty. How great and numerous are Your ways!

In the morning we will seek Jesus. In the night watches we will meditate on Jesus.

I love You God! I love You Jesus! How great You are!

Truth, mercy and justice belong to You. Wisdom and understanding are Yours. Knowledge and patience are Yours.

How great is the Lord? Tell me how great is the King of Israel?

God will judge the world in righteousness, for a short work upon the earth will God make.

Listen to our prayers, Lord Jesus. Be attentive to the prayers of Your saints.

Yahweh, You are awesome!

Yahweh, You are awesome!

Yahweh, You are awesome!

Remember Your servants Abraham, Isaac and Jacob. Remember Your covenant with Your faithful servants.

We love You Lord God. We need You in our daily lives. We need Your divine guidance.

Redeem Israel Elohim, Redeem Israel Elohim, Redeem Israel Elohim.

In the name of the
Father, the Son and
the Holy Ghost

Amen and Amen
Copyright © 2008

A Prayer of Beauty

A prayer by Mark Berryhill

God of mercy, God of love, God of justice, God of wrath. How excellent and terrible is Your name throughout all the earth! Your ways are past finding out.

Into the light, and out of darkness. A King slow to anger and slow to wrath.

Not by His power, or by His might, but with His Spirit, He will write the greatness of His Word in our minds.

As the beauty of the changing leaves in Autumn, so is the beauty of our God.

As the birth of a newborn child, so is the everlasting beauty of our God.

As the hen broods over her chicks, so is God over His children.

Beauty surpassed by description, beauty surpassed by human words, so is the beauty of our Lord.

Light, incomprehensible light, is where our Lord Jesus lives and reigns. And though He is higher than the Heavens, His Spirit dwells within His children.

My friend, my Savior, our King. No greater love has any man than to lay down his life for his friends.

Lord Jesus, take me home to where You are. Take me home.

Lord Jesus, we will seek love, truth, peace, harmony and gentleness.

Lord Jesus, I know You will never leave me nor forsake me. I belong to You.

Wisdom and love are from the Most High. The Lord possessed wisdom at the creation. Before the mountains were brought forth, or ever the earth was, wisdom dwelt with the LORD.

Answer our prayers Most High. Be alert and attentive to our cries.

You are strength. You are love. You are beauty. You are our all in all.

Mold us with Your skillful hands Lord Jesus. Mold us as the potter the clay.

Arise, arise, arise O Lord! Out of Your slumber, arise O Lord!

A God of war, a God of peace. Great and dreadful is His name. Loved and feared, Jesus reigns.

Beauty. God is beauty. When a friend has nowhere to turn, and you lend a hand, beauty and righteousness walk hand in hand.

Jesus is His name. Beauty and righteousness walk hand in hand.

In the name of the
Father, the Son and
the Holy Ghost

Amen and Amen
Copyright © 2008

From a Faithful Lord

A prayer by Mark Berryhill

Father, in You we live, we move and we have our being. O Lord, why do You hide when we need You the most?

As the laughter of a child, so is the beauty of my King's unfailing love.

As the older brother protects the younger sister, so is the faithfulness of our Lord.

Whether happy or sad, surrounded by many or few, rich or poor, my God, my Lord will never leave me.

I am never alone. Though unseen, the Lord never leaves His child.

The covenant of my King is faithfulness to death, for no greater love has any man than to lay down his life for his friends.

Whether traveling far or near, an invisible, eternal King is near.

Thanksgiving and thankfulness, thank You for creating us.

Thank You for the air that we breathe, for the food we eat and for the clothes we wear.

Most of all, thank You for the precious Lamb.

Pursing love. Pursing God. Pursing mercy, truth, justice, integrity, kindness and goodness. On these are where our minds will dwell.

O faithful LORD, help us in our time of need. Deliver us in our time of trial and temptation. Be attentive to our prayers, most High.

Thank You for the avenue of prayer, Lord God. Thank You for being attentive to our prayers.

More beautiful than the gentleness displayed by a mother toward her baby girl, so is the everlasting beauty of the King of kings. There is but one King, His name is Jesus.

Great and terrible is His name! Vengeance belongs to God!

Uprightness of heart, uprightness of mind, for vengeance belongs to the Lord.

A moment, a day or one hundred and twenty years when compared to eternity, what is a day or one hundred and twenty years?

We seek righteousness, holiness and godliness. We are bought with the price of the King.

Eternal love, eternal hope, eternal King, eternal One. Yahweh is His name.

Redeem Israel, my Lord, my King.

In the name of the
Father, the Son and
the Holy Ghost

Amen and Amen
Copyright © 2008

A Repentant Heart

A prayer by Mark Berryhill

Father, forgive me of the sins of my youth. Lead me in the path of righteousness, for Your great names sake.

Father, reach out with Your strong arm and carry these precious lambs.

Awake to righteousness, and sin no more Israel.

Love, mercy, kindness and gentleness: qualities of the King.

Protect these precious children, Lord God. Lead them in the pathways of righteousness and holiness. Guard them with Your mighty angels. Guide them with Your Holy Spirit.

Majestic are Your works! Glorify Your name throughout all the earth!

We walk in humility before the Great King.

Father, bless us with the Spirit of wisdom and love. Fill us with Your Holy Spirit! Teach us Your precepts. A nation of holy men and holy women. God's own people.

Lord Jesus, thank You for life. We love You and we adore You. Thank You for eternal victory.

All praise, glory, and honor to God the Father, the Lord Jesus Christ, and the Holy Ghost.

You are worthy Lamb of God. You alone are worthy.

Lord God, the earth is Yours, and all the fullness therein. We ask for You to be our Lord.

Glorify Your holy name throughout all the earth!

In the name of the
Father, the Son and
the Holy Ghost

Amen and Amen
Copyright © 2008

Jesus, the Light of the World

A prayer by Mark Berryhill

Lord Jesus, You are the light of the world. Glorify Your great and matchless name, Lord Jesus!

Lord Jesus, we praise You for having called us out of the darkness and into Your marvelous light.

We will run our race in Your great and marvelous light. We will run the race to win the prize.

The prize, our Lord, is for eternity. The prize, our Lord, is the Heaven that is higher than the Heavens. The prize, our Lord is You.

Lord Jesus, draw us near to You. Fill our hearts and minds with Your love and purity.

Fill us with Your great Word, my Lord, my God.

Loving kindness, gentleness and compassion: Jesus is His name.

God is love. God is life. God is light. We show our great love for You by keeping Your holy commandments, yet our eternal salvation is by Your blessed grace.

Worthy to be praised is the Lamb. Worthy to be praised is the Lamb of God. Holy, holy, holy, Lord God Almighty. Holy, holy, holy, Lord God Almighty.

In the name of the
Father, the Son and
the Holy Ghost

Amen and Amen
Copyright © 2008

Compassion, Mercy and Truth

A prayer by Mark Berryhill

Two absolute truths. God controls the rain and owns eternal life.

Rainbow upright, rainbow straightforward. Uprightness of heart, uprightness of mind. Soundness of mind and purity.

Can you describe the colors of the rainbow?

I reach for You, my Lord. I want to know my God.

Father, beauty and holiness belong to You. Teach us Your precepts.

Love, compassion, mercy and truth. Unfailing love. Faithful. True.

The faithfulness of my Father, the longsuffering of my Father, the love of my Father God.

Unfailing guidance from the Father of lights.

There is no fear, there is hope. There is God.

Mockingbird, blue jay and canary, where do you belong?

His love is beyond human comprehension. His love never abandons.

Blessed is this child of the King. Thankful is this child of the King.

Children are the delight of His heart. The children are His great rewards. Children are the joy of His heart. Children are the reason for life.

Ten more for me will do, my Lord.

We who walk in the light are God's possessions.

I ask, who is this great God that I love and fear? Who is this great Lord that I love and fear?

Jesus is His name. Son of the Most High is His name.

The Lord is Nathan's strength. The Lord is his great reward.

Abraham, Abraham, Evan called out. Abraham, Abraham, Evan called out.

Exalted Father. Father of a multitude. Abraham is his name.
Friend of the Most High God.

In the name of the
Father, the Son and
the Holy Ghost

Amen and Amen
Copyright © 2008

God as our Strength

A prayer by Mark Berryhill

Redeem Israel, O Lord. Redeem Israel, O Lord. Redeem Israel, O Lord.

Father, protect these precious children. Without You and Jesus in our daily lives, we are lost sheep without their Shepherd.

My King, our King. My Lord, our Lord. How great You are! Worthy is the Lamb.

Care for us while we are young and when we are old.

Father, love us. Come and heal this great land. Lead us in the pathways of righteousness, holiness and godliness for Your great name's sake.

Holy, holy, holy Lord God Almighty. Blessed is the Lord of hosts. Love, truth, mercy, kindness, compassion and integrity are His.

Love us, our Lord. Love us and mold us with Your skillful Hands. Write Your great Word in our hearts and in our minds.

Purity, virtue and self-control are the teachings of the great King. We will walk spotless and blameless before our Lord.

Grace and truth are from Jesus Christ. Grace and truth are from the King of kings.

Higher than the Heavens for my King. Higher than the Heavens is my King's love for me.

Farther than the east is to the west is the love of my King for me. Farther than the west is to the east is my love for my King.

Father, be attentive to my prayers. Open Your ears to my prayers, O Lord. Answer quickly, respond suddenly to the prayers of Your friend.

Grace and truth are from Jesus Christ. Grace and truth are from the King. Wisdom and love. Love and wisdom. Wisdom and love. Love and wisdom.

I love You my King and my Rock. I long to be with You and safe from harm. We love You, our King. We long to be with You and safe from harm.

Father, take notice of the elderly man. Help the elderly man, my Lord. When I see him again, I will tell the elderly man about my friend.

Patient, loving, kind, gentle, longsuffering and joyful is the King.

Father, we love You! Jesus we adore You! Spirit we need You, in all that we do!

Meditate on the Word day and night. Meditating on the Word day and night is our joy and delight.

Christ Jesus, Nathan is Yours. Evan is Yours. To Shepherd and Bishop our souls is His work.

The burden is too heavy for me to carry my Lord, I lift it up to You, my God.

I am free of guilt and free of worry because of a King. The blood of a precious Lamb makes me more pure than the whitest snow.

Heaven is His throne. The earth is His footstool. The Governor of Israel eternally reigns.

In God's hand is the breath of life. In God's hand is Heaven and hell.

We are walking in love and righteousness, what shall we fear? Our God leads us with righteousness of heart.

By the strength of His right hand will He lead His chosen. Bondage and slavery for too many years. By the strength of His right hand He will lead His children home.

In the light God reigns eternally. Yes, in the light God will dwell forevermore.

I love God and my God loves me. Uprightness of heart is mine, not of mine own, but a gift from the Father of lights.

O Lord, rewarding are Your ways. Self-control of flesh and Spirit are a blessing from the King.

I am blameless and spotless in the flesh and Spirit because I fear the great King.

In a moment, in the twinkling of an eye, dissolved the universe will be. Heaven or hell, where will you spend eternity?

Eternal love, eternal separation, freedom of choice is given from the King of kings.

Obedience or disobedience, freedom of choice is from the King of kings.

Father, thank You for life and for love. Thank You for Your amazing grace.

Righteousness, holiness and godliness are the pathways of our King.

Purity in the flesh is a wonderful reward of the King.

When we truly love our King, the commandments of the King are kept.

Loveliness, kindness, gentleness, compassion, truth, mercy and integrity are but a few words that compliment our Lord.

Wrath and vengeance belong to the Lord.

In the name of the
Father, the Son and
the Holy Ghost

Amen and Amen
Copyright © 2008

In the Night Watches with the Lord

A prayer by Mark Berryhill

In the night watches, I will call unto the Lord. He will hear my prayer. He is faithful and true.

My Father, my God, envelope me with Your majesty! Enlighten the world with Your power!

Blue, orange, rocks and plants You are Creator of all.

You are our love, our life and our all in all. We will sing praises unto Jesus in the night watches.

O Lord, we have many questions for You.

Holy Spirit, how great You are! Lead us with Your Holy Spirit our Lord, our King.

Not by His power or His might, but by His Spirit He will lead us home.

Holy, holy, holy, Lord God Almighty. How great and marvelous are Your works!

Thank You for the beauty of the nights. Thank You for the brilliance of the shinning stars. How many stars are there, Lord God? God calls them by name each night, and yet man cannot number the stars.

Faithful and true is the King of kings. Faithful and true is the Lord of lords.

Jesus we love You! Father, we love You! Holy Spirit, we love You!

How great and marvelous are Your works my Lord and my God!

How sweet is the sleep of the laboring man. How sweet is the sleep of this blessed man.

I am a child of the King and so can you be. Follow the King.

Heaven and hell are the Great King's. I will fear Him all of my days. Oh, how I love my King.

Justice and integrity belong to God.

Father, in Your hand is my life, my breath and my future. How wonderful it is to be a child of the King.

In all I will praise the King. On Him I will lean.

Freedom, how great is the freedom Jesus provides His children? In You I will hope. In You we will trust.

Lead us in the pathways of virtue, purity and holiness. Teach Your children Your Word, Almighty God.

Write Your Word in our hearts and in our minds. Keep us in the Word.

Hallelujah to the Lord of hosts. Hallelujah to the Lord of the armies of Heaven.

Onward Christian soldiers, let us be transformed into the likeness of Christ.

I love You Lord God Almighty. Lead me by Your hand. Remember Your servants Abraham, Isaac and Jacob. Remember Your great covenant with Your servant Abraham.

Love us Lord God. Thank You for today.

Life and death are in the hand of God. How important are our words and our works to God?

The battle belongs to the Lord. Love us Lord God. We need Your love and guidance in our daily lives.

Listen and consider the peacefulness and quietness we receive while meditating on God. Stay with me at all times, O Lord.

Love, compassion and kindness belong to the Lord. Vengeance and wrath also belong to God.

Teach the people Your Word, Almighty God.

Jesus said, "Follow me, and I will make you fishers of men."[8] They became fishers of men.

The rain belongs to God. Our eternal destiny rests in His right hand.

Lord, I love Your precepts. It is a joy to walk in holiness, righteousness and uprightness of heart.

Father, thank You for being holy. Thank You for Jesus.

What is beauty? Tell me wise men, what is beauty? Our children are God's great reward.

---

[8] Matthew 4:19

Stay near to me O Lord. Near to me please stay. I will worship God each day and for eternity.

Arise, my Lord. Arise Great Warrior. Be attentive to the cries of Your children.

Pure, undefiled and spotless until death or until the return of the King.

Excitement, joy and love are but a few words that compliment our God.

In the name of the
Father, the Son and
the Holy Ghost

Amen and Amen
Copyright © 2008

A Prayer to the Eternal One

A prayer by Mark Berryhill

Father, they ask who You are. They ask who is God? Father, they do not realize what Your servant Daniel spoke about You. In Your mighty hand the very breath of life is held.

You are our sustenance and our provision. Father, how is it possible for us to long for You and desire You in the manner we long for You?

Father, where is Your great love? Father, we need for You to be our God.

In health I will praise God and in sickness I will praise God.

Father help us to be as You are. Give us the qualities of virtue, purity and love.

The Spirit of love and the Spirit of wisdom is my prayer to You, my Lord and my King.

Not only for me, O God, but for each of us who need You so much.

Purity, holiness and godliness: these are the qualities the children of God seek.

Father, stay near to me. When You are near, I am more confident.

Father, humility, kindness, gentleness and compassion are the qualities we long for.

Father, make us to be like Jesus. Transform us into the likeness of Your Son. We want to be men and women of God, men and women of the Most High. Pure, holy and righteous. We will be like our King.

How beautiful are You? How great are You my Lord? How much love do You possess my God?

You are ours and we are Yours, servants and saints of the King of Israel.

There is no fear of life nor death when one belongs to God.

Love us, O Lord. Love us with Your unfailing love. Walk us in the pathways of righteousness and holiness.

Some people ask, "who is God?" without realizing they were formed in the mother's womb with His hands.

How great are You my Lord God? How great is the King of kings?

The day of the Lord, we will know the greatness of the eternal God. In a moment, in the twinkling of an eye, we will know how great the Almighty is.

There is no greater joy in all the world than worshipping the Lamb of God. There is no greater fulfillment in all the world than seeking Jesus Christ.

Love us more Lord God. Love us the way You demand to be loved.

Holy, holy, holy Lord God Almighty! Holy is our God.

In the night I will pray unto my Lord. I will sing and praise my God. Why am I in love with my God?

We are pure and undefiled in the eyes of God provided we walk in the light of Christ. Don't you know the blood of the Lamb washes away our sins provided we walk in obedience?

He has called us out of darkness and into His marvelous light. Therefore, in the light we will dwell.

O Lord, how great and matchless is Your holy name!

Within His hand is life; within His hand is eternal life.

Have you put on the King? Have you repented and been baptized into the King?

Lead us Lord God. Lead us in the pathways of righteousness and holiness for Your great names sake.

Holy as the child sings out. Listen Father, holy the child sings out.

Eternal love. Eternal life. Jesus Christ is His name.

Obedience to the King. There is but one choice, obedience to the King!

Victory has been won and is owned by the King!

Teach us to love You with all of our being, our Lord, our God and our King.

As the gentle falling rain, so is the way my King gently leads me home.

O Lord God, write Your great Word in our hearts and in our minds.

Anxious in nothing except for death, thus I can go and be with the King. The King prevails.

How great is the Lord? Can you tell me, how great is the Lord?

In the name of the
Father, the Son and
the Holy Ghost

Amen and Amen
Copyright © 2008

God's own Children

A prayer by Mark Berryhill

Heaven is His and the earth is His. How great is the Lord? God is possessor of all.

I ask God, "Why do You continue, Lord God?" Then I see a child who loves His God.

I ask God, "Why do You continue, Lord God?" Then I see a child who loves her God.

We see living waters that are aqua and clear in color and skies of blue and white, pure white as white can be.

We will no longer thirst; our Lord will bless us with living water.

The King knows His children are we who love him and we who obey Him. We are God's own children.

Pure, holy and spotless are the King's children. Pure, holy and spotless are the King's children.

Father, love us the way You demand us to love You. Please love us the way You demand to be loved.

God reigns in the beauty of holiness, righteousness and judgment upon the mountains of God.

Rivers of water. We have seen rivers of living water and we will see Jesus rule over the universe in righteousness.

Help us to walk in the Spirit all of the days of our lives, Lord God.

The Lamb was slain before the foundation of the world. God prepared Heaven for His children before the foundation of the world.

We walk in righteousness, holiness and godliness for we follow the hand of God.

In the name of the
Father, the Son and
the Holy Ghost

Amen and Amen
Copyright © 2008

By God's own Power

A prayer by Mark Berryhill

As the newborn child cries for the comfort of her mother's arms, so I fret about my God.

He is invisible, He is beautiful, He is holy and righteous. He is the King, eternal and immortal.

Dust to dust, each of us goes in the way of all the earth, dust to dust. No man has power over His death.

We will seek the eternal King. We love and obey our Lord.

As suddenly as the lightening flashes across the sky, so will we meet our Maker.

Thunder, the voices of God. Lightning, the arrows of His army. Boanerges, Peter, James and John the sons of thunder.

Love, humility, kindness, gentleness, holiness, goodness and righteousness are but a few words that describe our King.

Clear water, crystal clear water, aqua in color and there are white caps as JEHOVAH commands the wind.

Time is in His powerful hand. Peter, James and John friends of the Most High.

Mercy, truth, justice, integrity and honesty, words that describe a faithful King.

Clear, crystal clear water, living waters, eternal life.

We all will meet Jesus. Obey the commandments of God.

Grace and truth are from Christ Jesus, but not as a cloak for unrighteousness. "For if we sin willfully after that we have received the knowledge of the truth, there remaineth no more sacrifice for our sins, but a certain fearful looking for of judgment and fiery indignation, which shall devour the adversaries."[9]

Father, we love Jesus and we need You. Spirit, we praise You.

---

[9] Hebrews 10:26-27

God the Father, the Lord Jesus Christ, and the Holy Spirit, the Blessed Trinity.

In laughter and in sadness, in joy and in sorrow, in love and in hate, in harmony and in difficulty, we are never alone, God is always with us.

Jesus is my friend. Within God's children is the Kingdom of Heaven.

By the strength of His right arm, He will deliver His children to their Heavenly home.

Walking in the Spirit. It is a joy to live righteously!

Discipline, patience and work are gifts and blessings from a faithful Father.

Abba, Father. The children are Your great reward. Be faithful to the children Lord God.

Lord of Hosts is His name. Lord of the armies of Heaven consider. Is God afraid?

I love God. I was a straying sheep He brought safely into the fold.

Father, comfort the needy. Bless them and cradle them in Your bosom.

Lord God, help us to walk blameless before You all of the days of our lives.

A vapor, a shadow and a mist so are the days of man.

Lord God, prove me, try me. The reins of the hearts of men are in the Supreme One's hand.

Day and night we meditate on Your Holy Word.

I pray for love and wisdom, Lord God. Bless these beautiful children with love and wisdom.

It is fun seeking the King. When I think I have found Him, He has moved.

Love without jealousy, pure hearts without bitterness.

Father, we seek love and not hate. We seek righteousness and holiness, not unrighteousness and uncleanness.

By God's right hand the universe is sustained. By the power of His holy arm we exist.

We will meet Jesus Christ. Uprightness of heart and uprightness of mind are blessings from God.

Happiness, joy, purity, virtue, temperance, brotherly love and compassion are also blessings from the Messiah.

The air we breathe, the food we eat and where we sleep, all are from God.

Praiseworthy is the King. Praiseworthy is Jesus our Lord. Thank You for loving us, Lord Jesus.

Pour out Your love on me, Lord God. Love and wisdom are gifts from above.

Little lambs, little sheep, the King knows who belongs to Him. Gently, the King leads His children home.

Christ is love and beauty. Can you smell the scent of the gentle falling rain?

Righteousness or unrighteousness, God gives freedom of choice. Heaven for a reward. Hell for punishment.

Mount Zion is the mountain of God. All of the mountains are Gods.

As a brother gently spoke rivers of water, rivers of water are by God's right hand.

O Lord, how great and majestic is Your universe! How beautiful are the works of Your fingers!

Love us, Lord God. Love us and lead us Lord Jesus.

Prepare Your children's the bride of Christ Most High. Prepare Your children our God, our King.

In the name of the
Father, the Son and
the Holy Ghost

Amen and Amen
Copyright © 2008

Laughter and Joy

A prayer by Mark Berryhill

I have found my LORD to be a bit of a showoff, but after considering the matter, I realize that when everything in Heaven and earth belongs to Him, a showoff our LORD can be.

O Lord, how laughter heals the soul. O Lord, how great are Your precepts!

God knows how to deliver His own. He came to seek and save that which was lost, not the righteous.

Abba, what will Heaven be like? How beautiful will it be? O Lord keep us in Your Word. There is love without end for all who love and obey the Lord Jesus.

Hell and destruction are reserved for the ungodly, unrighteous and unholy. Yes, if the righteous scarcely be saved, what about the ungodly?

Wisdom and love. Love and wisdom. Eternal life is the goal. We are Spirit and God's own worship Him in Spirit and in truth.

Train us to be godly, my God. Teach us to be like Jesus. I pray that You will bless children with love and wisdom.

We are Yours. Love us. Deliver Your people Israel, Lord God.

In the name of the
Father, the Son and
the Holy Ghost

Amen and Amen
Copyright © 2008

As the Potter and the Clay

A prayer and inspirational by Mark Berryhill

O Lord, how we love You! His righteousness we will seek. His greatness we will know. Bind love, mercy and truth on the table of our hearts dear Lord.

Remember us who are in need Lord God. The King of kings is faithful and true.

Thunder, glorious thunder, rain and arrows of lightning are from the Most High.

Great and matchless is His name! O Lord, how great is Your name throughout all the earth!

Tenderness, gentleness and kindness are from above. The child came and completed the work of the Father.

The great King showed us the way. Jesus lived the perfect life. Our example to follow has been demonstrated.

O Lord, how great and marvelous is Your Holy Bible! We praise You and thank You for Your Holy Word!

Thunder, rain and arrows of lightning are from the Most High. O Lord, teach us Your precepts.

Rivers of water, we are blessed of the King.

Humility, compassion, loveliness, godliness and peacefulness are words of greatness. O Lord, hear our prayers, be attentive to our prayers.

Answer quickly Your servant's prayers. Thank You for answering prayer our Lord and our God.

Heaven is beauty beyond description. Heaven waits for the children of the King. Yes, His children's names are written in the Lamb's Book of Life.

Father, love us and mold us with Your hands as the potter molds the clay.

O Lord, I marvel at Your greatness! In Your great hand is life and breath and eternal life!

Yes, we are Spirit and yes our days pass as quickly as Your arrows of lightning dart through the night sky.

O Lord have mercy on my soul. Forgive me of the sins of my youth.

Lead me in righteousness, my Lord and my King.

Can you hear the laughter of the child; do you see the picture of God's children? The child is the very reason for life.

Throughout all the earth, God will be feared! In His hand is Your life and mine.

Humility, gentleness and kindness, words that describe but a few qualities of our Lord.

O Lord, our LORD, give us wisdom and give us love. Lead us with Your Holy Spirit, our Lord and our King.

In the name of the
Father, the Son and
the Holy Ghost

Amen and Amen
Copyright © 2008

36

Prove us and try our Heart's O Lord

A prayer by Mark Berryhill

Why would You give Your life for a sinner like me, my Lord and my God?

Prove us and try our hearts, our Lord and our King.

Father, come and heal this great nation, my Lord and my King. We are Yours and You are ours; lead us in Your righteousness.

Uprightness of heart, the Lord is a buckler to the upright of heart.

Deliver us great King. Redeem Your people Israel, my Lord and my eternal King.

In the name of the
Father, the Son and
the Holy Ghost

Amen and Amen
Copyright © 2008

Jesus Reigns for He is God's Son

A prayer by Mark Berryhill

O Lord our LORD, thank You for today. Thank You for another day to worship You.

The Lord will be exalted! The LORD reigns! Yahweh is His name!

J.A.H., JEHOVAH, Jesus. Where is there comfort? Where is there peace? I will rest in the strength of the Almighty.

God is love. I ask, can you sustain the nations by the strength of your right hand?

Father, we love You. Jesus, we adore You. Spirit, we need You.

In righteousness and in truth, He will redeem His people Israel.

The Governor of nations is His name, King of kings and Lord of lords.

Father, protect my friend Shawn. Father, guard him with the strength of Your right hand.

Purity, love and holiness, it must be the intervention of the Divine.

Teach us Your ways, our Lord. Write Your great Word on our hearts and minds.

Teach us to serve You all the days of our lives.

The fear of the Lord is clean and pure. May I fear the Lord all of my days.

The fear of the Lord is the beginning of knowledge. Be wise and fear the Lord.

Lord God, how high are the Heavens? Lord God, how great is Your love for Your people?

Jesus reigns. Jesus is the King. Yes, there is a reason He is the King. Son of the Most High is His name.

O Father, bless the children. Mold them with Your skillful hands. You, our Lord are our all in all.

Guide us in Your righteousness. Lead us in Your holiness.

Higher than the Heavens and deeper than the ocean is my love for my King.

We will seek the Lord! We will extol the Lord! The LORD our King will be exalted.

A peculiar people are the people of God, a nation consisting of holy men and holy women.

How great You are, O Lord! How great You are my God, and my King!

From my mother's womb You were with me, yes, my God is always with me.

Mercy and truth, bind them upon the table of our hearts, O LORD and our King.

In the name of the
Father, the Son and
the Holy Ghost

Amen and Amen
Copyright © 2008

The God of Light, Love and Life

A prayer by Mark Berryhill

The clouds are the dust of God's feet.

He is light. He is love. He is my life. I will praise and exalt my Lord, my King!

He is love, beauty, purity and holiness. We will seek the face of the King.

We who love Him and obey Him belong to the King.

We are bought at the price of a King. Glorify the King in body and in Spirit!

All the days of my life I will fear my God. All the days of my life I will love my God.

No man has power over death. Glorify the King in body and in Spirit! As many as You that have been baptized into Christ have put on Christ.

Jesus, we love You! Jesus, we adore You! Jesus, we need You! A strong tower and refuge for the poor and afflicted is our LORD the King.

Keep yourself blameless and spotless until the King returns.

As graceful and effortless as the deer glides over the fence, so is the gentleness with
which the King leads His sheep home.

> In the name of the
> Father, the Son and
> the Holy Ghost
>
> Amen and Amen
> Copyright © 2008

Blessings for God's Children

A prayer by Mark Berryhill

Draw near to us our Lord and our King. Be near to me my LORD and my King.

Teach us to trust in You with our whole heart. Teach us to hope in You with all of our heart.

Live daily with the King. Life is a joy when one walks daily with the King.

Grace and truth came by Jesus Christ. We who love God will keep His commandments.

Father, keep us in prayer. Teach us to commune with You in our daily lives.

Holy, holy, holy, holy LORD God Almighty. Worthy to be praised is the Lamb of God.

Father, I pray that You will bless these precious children with Your love and Your wisdom.

In the name of the
Father, the Son and
the Holy Ghost

Amen and Amen
Copyright © 2008

As the Birth of a Newborn Baby Boy

A prayer by Mark Berryhill

O Lord our Lord, how excellent is Your name throughout all the earth!

Father, let me know who You are. Try my heart, prove me, and love me.

Father, when I pray to You, hear my prayers, my God and my King.

O Lord, give me an honest and pure heart.

The nations will glorify the LORD! The nations will magnify the LORD!

We will walk in Your righteousness, O Lord. We will walk in truth and with uprightness of heart.

Awake to righteousness and sin no more! Eternity is forevermore!

Do you remember a man named Noah? Do you remember Sodom and Gomorrah?

Awake to righteousness and sin no more!

Warn your friends to sin no more! Warn your friends to sin no more! Warn your friends to sin no more!

O Lord, thank You for Jesus and His blood that makes us whiter than snow. Lord Jesus, thank You for the sacrifices You paid for our sins.

We will worship I AM THAT I AM, in the beauty of holiness.

In Spirit and in truth we will worship our King. Bind mercy and truth upon the table of my heart, my Lord and my King.

He is unfailing love, my friend and Creator of mankind. Why is man called man? Why is woman called woman?

At the resurrection of the just, those who have done the will of God go home; those who have continued in disobedience will also go to their home.

Love, compassion, kindness and goodness are four words which accurately state a few qualities of our Lord.

Think in beauty, virtue and purity.

Try our hearts, O God. Prove us. You hold the reigns. Try our hearts, my Lord and my King. Prove us.

There are no words to describe how much we are loved by our King.

Give us uprightness of heart and uprightness of mind. Walk us in Your righteousness O Lord.

He is gentle and true. Lord Jesus, teach us to love You in the manner You love us.

I ask the Lord, Oh Lord, why do You continue? Then I remember the birth of a newborn baby boy.

How great are Your ways, my Lord and my King? How great are Your ways?

Listen before speaking. Listen before speaking. What was said?

Be quick to hear, slow to speak and slow to wrath. Vengeance belongs to the Lord.

Be harmless as a dove, and as wise as a serpent.

O LORD our God, there is a world to evangelize. Let us go to work. Love us. Stay close to us. Draw near to us and protect us.

What will we fear? God is our Father.

Concentrate on these qualities of Christ; think on humility, gentleness and goodness.

Children are His great reward. He chose the greatest reward.

I love You, my Lord, and my God. Thank You for the children You blessed me with. Lead them in the pathways of righteousness and holiness. Teach them Your precepts. Write Your Word in their hearts and in their minds.

Transform us into the likeness of the King.

Give us discipline, love, patience and virtue.

The LORD reigns. The earth is His. The inhabitants are His. The gold and silver are His. The home is prepared and Jesus says it is the Father's good pleasure to give His children the kingdom.

How can a man stand without God's Word written in his heart? Tell me if you can, how can a man stand without God's Word written in his heart?

Life is short. Life is eternity. Live in the Spirit and not in the flesh.

When I called to my God, He heard my cry. He came down from Heaven to heal His wayward child.

How great You are my Lord and my God! O Lord, how great are Your marvelous signs and wonders!

He bowed the Heavens and came down to redeem His children Israel. In His mighty hand are life, death and eternal victory.

Victory belongs to the Lord. Give praise to the Lord. Exalt the Lord. There is thunder, rain, arrows of lightning and wind. The LORD is near.

Lord Jesus, thank You for my family. Thank You for Your faithfulness to me.

Teach us to love You with total abandonment of ourselves. Even if You slay me, Lord, I will trust in You.

Can you see the gentle waters softly dancing against the seashore? Tranquility, silence and softness are gifts from the King.

O LORD, redeem Your people Israel. O LORD, heal Your great people Israel.

Thank You for healing me, my Lord and my God. Father, cause my thoughts to be always on You.

Let me be continually praising Your name. Cause us to be happy, content and lacking in nothing. He is love and beauty. I will seek Your face, my God.

He is faithful and true God, Jesus and also my earthly dad. Faithful and true.

In the name of the
Father, the Son and
the Holy Ghost

Amen and Amen
Copyright © 2008

The King Approaches

A prayer by Mark Berryhill

Father, redeem Israel. Heal this great land for Your great names sake.

God is love. Thank You Lord Jesus for answering the prayers of this poor man.

Listen to me all you saints, have mercy toward the needy. Do you not know that by doing so, you have loaned to the Lord?

Justice and mercy are more valued than sacrifice to God.

Love us the way You desire to be loved, my God. Open Your heart and love us.

Lead and direct us in Your righteousness. Teach this great people to walk in the purity of Your Spirit, my God and my King.

Father, be with the sick. Comfort them as only You can. Father, protect Your children Israel.

Who are God's children? Tell me, who belongs to the most High?

Warn your friends! Warn your loved ones? The King approaches! The King approaches!

Feed the lambs you elders. Feed the lambs you elders. Feed the lambs you elders.

Are you a fisherman among men? Are you a disciple of Christ?

Reward follows obedience while punishment follows disobedience.

Grace and mercy came by Jesus Christ. The law came by God's servant Moses.

Hear my prayers my God. Open Your ears to my prayers. Be attentive to our prayers my God, and my all.

O Lord our LORD, how great and wonderful is Your name! We marvel at the works of Your fingers, the sun, moon and stars. The great mountains and the great sea.

Rivers of water are by the right hand of the Mighty One.

Jesus, thank You for today. Father prepare Your people as the bride of Your Son. Have us watching and ready for the King.

Blessed is the nation whose LORD is God. Blessed is the earth whose LORD is God.

Consider life, love, justice, mercy and compassion. His name is Jesus Christ.

In the name of the
Father, the Son and
the Holy Ghost

Amen and Amen

A Prayer of Love

A prayer by Mark Berryhill

Rich and poor meet together; the Lord is Maker of us all.

Sell what you have, give it to the poor and follow the King.

Faith, perseverance, patience, kindness and humility. His name is Yahweh.

I dare say who would name His children the fruit of the womb but the Most High?

They are His great reward. They are the reason Christ is King. In Him we will all trust.

In life and death, love and hate, laughter and sadness, peace and war, rain and drought, God is unchanging and the LORD of hosts.

We pursue the King. We love the King. We fear the King.

Thank You for Your blood, my King that continually cleans us from all sin, as we walk in the light.

Bright and shinning stars are those who turn many to righteousness.

Repent, you sinners. Confess the King, you sinners. Be baptized in His name and let us be cleansed from the sins of our youth.

In the light and obedience we will walk hereafter.

How many colors are in Your great rainbow, my Lord and my King?

How great and marvelous are Your signs and wonders! We long for You in purity, our Lord and our King.

Thank You for Your great Word. Teach us Your Word, our Lord and our King. Teach us Your great Word.

Keep us holy, blameless, spotless and ready for the return of the Lamb.

Abba, Abba come heal this great land. I AM THAT I AM can do all things.

As the children need both father and mother, so we all need You, our Lord and our God.

Virtue, purity, righteousness and holiness are qualities we will pursue.

When I cried, He heard. When I sang, He sang. When I laugh, He laughs. When we cry, He cries. O Lord our LORD, how great You are!

He is love so amazing and so kind. Teach us Your Word, our LORD and our King.

The fear of the LORD is the beginning of wisdom. How long, my LORD is eternity?

In the name of the
Father, the Son and
the Holy Ghost

Amen and Amen
Copyright © 2008

For the Ones we Love

A prayer by Mark Berryhill

Lord Jesus, thank You for the beauty of the days, for the air we breathe, for the food we eat and for the clothes we wear.

Lord Jesus, thank You for our families, our parents, our mates, our children, our brothers and our sisters.

Lord Jesus, thank You for never leaving us. Thank You for being faithful to me.

Lord Jesus, thank You for a young boy named Nathan.

Lord Jesus, thank You for a young girl named Evan.

What a joy they are to You and me.

Father, You truly are love, joy, peace and hope. We are Yours and You our Lord are ours.

Lord Jesus, prepare Your people as Your bride. Lord Jesus, prepare Your great people as Your bride.

Lord, You bring laughter and smiles, joy and happiness, love and caring.

And You Lord God, what will we do with You?

Open Your heart, Lord God, and love Your children the way You desire to be loved. We are Yours and You are ours. You are our LORD and our God.

Praise the Lord all you saints! Glorify the Lord! Exalt His name with me! It is a joy to praise our King.

In the name of the
Father, the Son and
the Holy Ghost

Amen and Amen
Copyright © 2008

49

In the Name of the Lord

A prayer by Mark Berryhill

Lord God, we love You and we need You.

Be our Father, Lord God. Carry us by the strength of Your mighty right hand.

Bless us and love us. Guide and direct us in the pathways of righteousness and holiness for Your great names sake!

Concentrate on truth, mercy and justice. The Lord will deal with the liar and the fornicator.

Let us provide for the needy, care for the widows and keep ourselves spotless from the world.

What is wisdom and knowledge? Turning those who will to righteousness.

Meditate on patience, discipline and love. O Lord our LORD, how great and marvelous are the works of Your hands!

You truly are unfailing love. You were faithful unto death. Faithful and true is the King of kings.

Put within me a clean heart, O Lord. Create within me a new Spirit.

Come and heal this great people, my Lord and my King.

He is invisible and eternal. He is the only wise God.

Great is Your loving kindness, my Lord and my God! Great are Your tender mercies!

Father, thank You for Jesus. Jesus, thank You for loving us.

God is merciful and mighty! God is terrible and dreadful! Remember Your servants, O Lord. Remember Your saints. Our Lord and our King.

You are beauty, love and holiness beyond description. Yes, the beauty of true holiness.

Wisdom and love are for the Most High. Bless all of these great children with Your wisdom and Your love Most High.

Can you picture clear living waters? Clear living waters are a gift from the King.

Warn your friends! Warn your friends! Awake to righteousness and sin no more!

Yes, weigh eternity. Yes, wise man, weigh eternity. Yes, wise woman, weigh eternity.

Love is from above. Love is from the Father of lights. He gave us the perfect gift, one baby boy, a precious bundle of joy.

Even though You slay me, I will trust in You, my Lord and my King.

All praise, glory and honor to God the Father, the Lord Jesus Christ and the Holy Ghost. Yes, all you people, exalt the name of the Lord with me.

You are our provision and our all in all.

God is a faithful friend. His name is Prince of Peace.

Life and death are in the hand of the King. Love Divine; fill us with Your Holy Spirit, my God.

We are forgiven, yes, but bought at the price of a King.

In the light is where we will dwell. The blood of the Lamb cleanses those who walk in the light.

He came to seek and save the lost. My friends, awake to righteousness and sin no more!

Can you smell the fresh cut grass? We are appreciative of the gift of smell.

As beautiful as the golden field with the morning dew, so is the faithfulness of God.

Think on humility and kindness. Train yourself to be godly. Transform us, our Lord and our God, into the likeness of Your Son.

In the name of the
Father, the Son and
the Holy Ghost

Amen and Amen
Copyright © 2008

Before Conception

A prayer by Mark Berryhill

Father, we love You, we adore You and we need You. You are our hope and our strength.

From before the time of conception, I was Yours. Before the time of conception, Nathan was Yours. Before the time of conception, Evan belonged to You.

I went astray in my youth, my Lord and my God, but You have shown me mercy and unfailing love.

I can never repay You, my God, nor can I repay parents as faithful as mine.

Lord Jesus, how great You are! I pray You will show mercy to Your people Israel.

Love us and mold us into what You knew Your people would become.

For we will be a nation of holy men and holy women; men and women who live in the Spirit, men and women who have chosen to keep themselves spotless and blameless.

Father, stay near to each one of us. Be our God. Be our strength and our strong tower.

Love, wisdom, beauty, purity, virtue, kindness and enduring faithfulness: qualities of the King.

O Lord, our LORD, how we long for You. We long to be with You in paradise, safe from hurt and harm. Abba, Father, I pray for Your divine intervention in the daily affairs of mankind.

Transform us into the likeness of Your Son, and our Savior Jesus.

In the name of the
Father, the Son and
the Holy Ghost

Amen and Amen
Copyright © 2008

Blessings and Laughter

A prayer by Mark Berryhill

Father, we love You! Why are You the way You are?

Father, why are we the way we are?

Father I pray that You will bless these precious children with Your love and your wisdom.

Lord Jesus, we must feed Your sheep Your great Word.

Purity and holiness is what we desire. Help us to keep ourselves unspotted from the world.

Father, thank You for Jesus. Jesus, thank You for loving us despite our weaknesses and shortcomings.

Lord God, we desire to know You. We long to be with You.

Lord God, thank You for Your Son and our Savior.

Feel the cool breeze during the night, God is near.

Father, the stars are magnificent tonight, brilliant blue, white and innumerable!

Your works are too marvelous for me! Father, how do You sustain all things? I know Lord God, yes I know, by the Word of God.

Lord Jesus, what are we going to do with Your Daddy? Thank You for the blessing of laughter my Lord and my King.

Feed the sheep Your great Word, Lord God.

We must begin teaching Your children Your Word from childhood.

Father, thank You for today! Thank You for the joy and blessings of a hard days work.

God is kindness, gentleness and humility. Write Your Word in our hearts and in our minds, Lord God.

Help us to keep Your commandments Lord God. Teach us Your precepts. Righteousness, holiness and godliness are the pathways we choose. Lord Jesus, place us in Your bosom as God has placed You in His.

You are the great Shepherd of our souls. Help and teach us to follow where You lead us each day.

Thank You for helping me to walk in the Spirit and not in the flesh. Thank You for forgiving me of the sins of my youth.

Thank You for marriage Lord God. Thank You for holy and righteous women.

Thank You for our children that bring us such indescribable joy and happiness.

In the name of the
Father, the Son and
the Holy Ghost

Amen and Amen
Copyright © 2008

Because of the Blood of the Lamb

A prayer by Mark Berryhill

Lord God, help those who are in need. Intervene in their lives, and be their Father.

Thank You for Jesus, Lord God. Thank You for His blood that continually washes our sins provided we walk in the light.

I will pursue love, kindness, compassion and charity. Lord God, teach us Your Word.

Blessed be the name of the Lord. The Lord taketh away and the Lord giveth.

Lord God, we need You and Jesus to be our LORD. Lead us in the pathways of righteousness and holiness.

Teach us to lean on You, and not on our own understanding. Teach us to deny ourselves, to pick up our cross daily and follow where You lead.

When I cried and needed You most, You were with me. Therefore, I will trust in You!

I ask You friends, have you seen two perfect upright rainbows? Great and marvelous are Your signs and wonders, Lord Jesus!

Father, we love You and Jesus. Draw near to us and help us teach our children Your Word.

Lord Jesus, thank You for my parents. Keep in mind the faithfulness they have shown unto me and so many others.

Lord God, remember loving kindness, longsuffering and tender mercies.

Thank You for giving me a mother who had me in church while I was growing up.

Thank You for the teachers that teach the Bible classes.

Lord Jesus, there is a world that desperately needs Your guidance and divine intervention.

Lord God, I pray You will give Your servants the Holy Spirit without measure. Teach us Your precepts and judgments.

Thank You for the coolness of the summer mornings and the coolness of the summer evenings.

Thank You for the beauty of the nights. We appreciate the gentle breezes and the brilliant stars.

Write Your Word on our hearts and minds, Lord Jesus. Help us to walk perfect and blameless before You the rest of our days.

Lord Jesus, how beautiful is Heaven? How glorious is Your home?

Love us and lead us Lord God. Be near to Your servants in our times of need.

Without You and Jesus, we are lost, Lord God. You are the Great Shepherd, lead us home.

Train yourself to be godly. Concentrate and meditate on God at all times so you will be prosperous.

Dwell on the eternal things and not on the temporal. The temporal pass away, the eternal is everlasting.

My Father, bless these precious children with the spirit of wisdom and love. Arise, O Lord. There isn't time for slumber.

In the name of the
Father, the Son and
the Holy Ghost

Amen and Amen
Copyright © 2008

Hand in Hand

A prayer by Mark Berryhill

O Lord our Lord, how great and terrible is Your name throughout all the earth!

God of war! God of peace!

He is Father, Son and Holy Spirit.

Hear O Israel the Lord our LORD is one LORD.

Lord Jesus, Lord God, stay near to us. Draw us near to Your side. Place these precious children in Your bosom.

Love, mercy, truth and compassion are the qualities of our King. These are the qualities we desire.

Father, when You decided to make children, You made a great decision.

Love them with all of Your heart, with all of Your soul and with all of Your mind.

Cherish them and mold them into the likeness of Your Son and our Savior.

Teach us to live by faith. Teach us Your statutes and commandments.

Father, except these precious children study Your Word daily, how will they know what a joy it is to walk with You hand in hand?

How will they know that they are to follow love, peace, compassion, mercy and truth except You teach them Your Word every day?

I AM THAT I AM, by Your hand all things are sustained, for in JEHOVAH we live, move and have our being.

In the name of the
Father, the Son and
the Holy Ghost

Amen and Amen
Copyright © 2008

Higher than the Heavens is His Love for Me

A prayer by Mark Berryhill

O Lord our LORD, when I consider the beauty of Your creation, I stand in awe!

Thank You for loving us. Thank You for creating us. Most of all, my God, thank You for Your Son.

Lord Jesus, we love You. Within our hearts and minds You have installed the desire for us to be holy.

Thank You for being holy, Lord God Almighty. Help us to follow in the footsteps of our King.

May we meditate on Your Word day and night. May You wash our minds with Your great Word.

Father, thank You for life. Thank You for eternal life.

Higher thank the Heavens and broader than from east to west is my Lord's love for me.

Father, Lord Jesus and Holy Spirit, be near to each one of us.

JEHOVAH is love, beauty, kindness, gentleness, compassion, judgment and justice.

The fear of the Lord is the beginning of wisdom, but fools despise knowledge.

Have you considered the length of eternity? Consider and walk hand in hand with your God.

Seek Him, love Him and call unto Him. He is so near. He is more near to you than you are to yourself.

Yes, seek diligently. He will never leave you, nor forsake you.

Is there a greater joy in life than walking daily with our God?

Is there a better and more faithful friend than our Lord?

The clothes you wear, the food we eat, the place you live, remember who provides these blessings.

Spend time with the Lord. Meditate on His Word. Pray without ceasing or else fall into temptation.

Dwell on purity, holiness and righteousness.

I know You will never leave me nor forsake me, Lord God.

The reason for life is the children. The reason for Jesus is the children.

Father, it is time for You, Jesus, and the Holy Spirit to go to work.

Father, we want You to be in our daily lives. We want Your divine guidance in our decision making. You made us where we have to have You, thank You.

Whether on a crisp, clear morning, or a hot summer day, my God is near me.

Father, I want to teach Your Word to the world.

"For I am not ashamed of the gospel of Christ: for it is the power of God unto salvation to every one that believeth; to the Jew first, and also to the Greek."[10]

How great is the Lord? Rather, how great are You my Lord and my King?

Friendship, laughter, peace, joy and children are the things the wise pursue.

The world rushes on. Take time to be holy. Let God transform us into the likeness of His Son.

Jesus, thank You for this great nation. Father, thank You for holy men and holy women who love You and keep Your commandments.

Help each of us to be shining stars for You.

People, hear my words. Write God's Word on the table of your hearts. Turn many to righteousness. Light the world for the King of kings!

In the name of the
Father, the Son and
the Holy Ghost

Amen and Amen
Copyright © 2008

---

[10] Romans 1:16

Hear our Prayers, O Lord

A prayer by Mark Berryhill

Can you hear the laughter of the children? Listen to the innocence of the laughter of the child at play.

"I can do all things through Christ which strengtheneth me."[11] You can do all things through Christ which strengtheneth you.

We are to prepare a people that walk in true holiness and true righteousness before the Lord.

Remember to keep yourself spotless, holy and undefiled before our great King.

Consider for a moment how quickly the time that we spend on earth passes by. Spend your time serving our Lord with prayer and fasting.

As the excitement a father feels when he hears the feet of his children patter running through the hallways, so is the excitement our Lord feels for those who love Him, serve Him and obey Him.

When I needed God the most, He heard me and answered my prayer. I cried out to the Lord and He answered me from His holy hill.

Father, teach us Your Word. Lord Jesus, write Your Word in our hearts and in our minds each day.

How do we define love? Love is to keep the commandments of the Lord.

Lord God, thank You for today. Lord Jesus, thank You for our children. Love them and watch over them all of the days of their lives. Stay near to each one of them.

Lord, we desire truth. We desire love, mercy and compassion. We need You. We need Your stern discipline.

---

[11] Philippians 4:13

How great is the Lord? How great is our faith in the blood of our Lamb?

We are whiter than snow before the King. Eye to eye, heart to heart, soul to soul, mind to mind and yet, whiter than snow.

Pure, holy and undefiled is the marriage bed to be kept.

God will judge the whoremonger and adulterer.

Brighter than the brightest of stars and whiter than the whitest of snow are those who turn many to righteousness.

Thank You Lord God for Your enduring love and mercy. It is more rewarding to be righteous and holy than unclean.

Never take Your love from us, our Lord and our God. Never forsake this great people Israel

Father, bless us with kindness, patience, longsuffering, gentleness, virtue, brotherly love and compassion.

How great is the LORD? How great is Yahweh, the God of Israel?

In the name of the
Father, the Son and
the Holy Ghost

Amen and Amen
Copyright © 2008

A Tear of Love. A Tear of Joy

A prayer by Mark Berryhill

Lord Jesus, thank You for providing work today. Thank You for the people who have helped those of us who were in need.

Young and tender, gentle and beautiful, light brighter than the brightest light, words that describes the beauty of the child.

Write Your Word on the table of our hearts, our Lord and our God.

A tear of love. A tear of joy. The child, an undeserved gift from the most High.

Young and tender. Kind and gentle. Innocent as a dove. Beautiful beyond human words, yes, the child, the gift.

Love exceeding light. Love exceeding the Heavens. The love God feels for His children.

God is provoked unto love and good works. We need you Lord, Lord God.

With You we can move mountains. You alone are life's sustenance. You alone, yet never alone.

We seek You because You loved us first. Continue to love us, our Lord and our God.

Higher than the Heavens and farther than east to west is my Father's love for His son's and daughter's.

Love is to keep the commandments of God. Love covers a multitude of sin.

Look at the child at play; consider the beauty of a child at play. Know that the eyes of the Lord never depart from the child at play.

He is Father, Son and Holy Ghost. Teach us the Word, my Lord and my King.

Mercy, justice and judgment. Heaven or hell. An eternal decision.

Consider eternal life with the Lord. Weigh eternal life with the Lord. Weigh eternal separation from the Lord.

My child, write God's Word on the table of your heart.

There is no greater joy in life than diligently seeking the righteous King.

Transform us into the likeness and brightness of Jesus, our Lord and our God.

Consider purity, virtue, honor, truth and discipline.

Wisdom, the beginning of knowledge is the fear of God.

We pursue godliness, holiness and righteousness.

Why does our Lord continue? What makes You reach beyond the Heavens, my Lord and, my God?

And I answer the fruit of the womb. The smile, the laughter and the innocence of God's child.

In the name of the
Father, the Son and
the Holy Ghost

Amen and Amen
Copyright © 2008

My Partner, my Friend

A prayer by Mark Berryhill

Work is a blessing so often taken for granted, and money is often used improperly.

Raise up laborers for Your harvest, Lord of the harvest.

Lord, You are our provision. You are our temporal and eternal provision. Creator, Savior, partner and friend, sustainer of Heaven and earth. God, You are great!

I enjoy looking over the mountain peaks, knowing You are near, feeling Your presence without seeing You, loving You even though You are invisible.

It is a pleasure to walk with You. Teach us to worship You in Spirit and in truth. Teach us to be like Jesus. Write Your commandments on the table of our hearts.

Self-restraint and self-discipline are from the Most High. Thank You for the Holy Spirit, Lord Jesus. Thank You.

Kindness, gentleness, compassion, mercy and truth are but a few words which complement our King.

As the doe gracefully races through the field, as the eagle soars through the firmament of Heaven, and as the leopard races for prey, beauty in motion created by God.

In the name of the
Father, the Son and
the Holy Ghost

Amen and Amen
Copyright © 2008

The Bride of Christ

A prayer of Mark Berryhill

When a person needs help, help them. When someone asks to borrow money, lend it to them.

Glorify God and Jesus in Your Spirit and in Your body. Prepare yourself as the bride of Christ. Train yourself to be godly. Study and meditate on God's Word. Pray without ceasing. Help the less fortunate. Give to the needy, in doing so, you have loaned to the Lord. He will repay with blessings unmeasured.

The time is at hand. Stop and consider how quickly life passes by. Those who do good will be raised and taken to Heaven. Those who have done evil will spend eternity in hell.

Walk in the light. Walk in accordance to the commandments.

Blessings and blessings, God is a God of eternal blessings.

Establish your faith in the blood of the Lamb. Settle your faith in the King. Know that He can do all things.

Father, Son and Holy Ghost, how great You are!

What is love? Do you know what love is? Love is the keeping of the commandments of God.

Why did God choose Abraham as the father of a multitude? Answer. God knew that he would teach his children THE WORD OF GOD.

Jesus, stay near us. Love us and mold us into the likeness and image of You. Love, mercy, truth, judgment, justice and unfailing faithfulness; Jesus is His name. he came to seek and save that which was lost. He is our Lord, our God and our King.

In the name of the
Father, the Son and
the Holy Ghost

Amen and Amen
Copyright © 2008

65

Have you Walked in the Valley of the Shadow of Death?

A prayer of Mark Berryhill

Have you seen the shadow of death? Have you walked hand in hand with God Almighty?

Never underestimate the love and wisdom God has given you. His Spirit dwells within His children and the Spirit of Jesus Christ and THE WORD OF GOD teach us all things according to the will of God.

Lord Jesus, I love You. Stay near to me and near to all of Your children. The children of God walk in the light. The children of God know THE WORD OF GOD.

Thank You for the sacrifice You paid for us, Lord Jesus. Thank You for the faith in God and discipline You exerted for Your children.

Father, we love You. We need You in our daily lives. Draw us near to Your Son Jesus. Love us, Lord God. Open Your heart to each one of us. Honesty, mercy and truth are our desire.

Can anyone say different, are our lives not but a shadow and a mist?

Glorify the Lord in your body and in the Spirit. Put away uncleanness. Walk uprightly and in the pathway of righteousness.

God blesses obedience. What is a blessing? The fruit of the womb, your children and mine.

In happiness or gloominess, in success or failure, the Lord's unfailing faithfulness never grows weary.

Teach us to be like Jesus, Lord God. Write Your Word on the table of my heart. Meditate daily on God's Word. Concentrate, examine and study our Creator's mind.

Turn many to a life of righteousness. Shine as the racing stars. O Lord, our LORD, how great and marvelous is all Your works! Love well. Hate evil.

The King is kindness, gentleness and compassion. Blessed be

the Lord of host's. blessed be the King of kings. Blessed be the Holy Ghost.

Who knows the mind of the Lord? Who were His counselors?

A baby boy, a child, a child was born, His name is Immanuel. God with us.

Consider precious little hands and precious little fingers and toes of Immanuel. His eyes remain eyes of love and innocence.

It is better to die than to be born, and better yet to have never been born. Oh Lord, my God, great is Your faithfulness! I ask you, have you lived your life to please the King?

He came to seek and save the lost. He is faithful. He is love. Walk in obedience, walk in the light, for as we were born we also will die.

Pray without ceasing. Pray with persistence. Pray and watch or you will fall into temptation.

Jesus, You are my love, my life and my all in all. Faithful parents, faithful friends, faithful brothers and sisters and faithful families are blessings of God. Love so amazing, loves gentle and love so kind.

Fear God and keep His commandments, for we will all explain our actions to Him.

In the name of the
Father, the Son and
the Holy Ghost

Amen and Amen
Copyright © 2008

Faith

A prayer of Mark Berryhill

She is as a beautiful rose, delicate and so exceeding tender.

She is as a soft falling dew, ever so refreshing and with a fragrance of honeysuckle.

She is a perfect example to all who know her; she is a daughter of the Great Jehovah.

She is a faithful wife, and she is a loving mother.

One of her many names is faith.

In the name of the
Father, the Son and
the Holy Ghost

Amen and Amen
Copyright © 2008

God of Israel

A prayer of Mark Berryhill

The beautiful little girl is clothed in a dress designed for the very princess she is.

The beautiful little girl has long black curly hair and a smile that makes her God's heart leap with joy.

The beautiful little girl in but a moment of time will have her own beautiful daughter.

The beautiful little girl is a daughter of the Great Jehovah, and she is the apple of His eye.

How great is the God of Israel?

In the name of the
Father, the Son and
the Holy Ghost

Amen and Amen
Copyright © 2008

His Love for the Child

By Mark Berryhill

Table of Contents

As Omega

A song of Mark Berryhill

If you die this day, where will you spend eternity? Have you been baptized into our Lord Jesus? Are you walking in the light of Christ?

Concentrate on the eternal, and not the temporal. Fix your eyes on the Lord.

Love Him, worship Him and serve Him with all of your being.

He loves us so. He is my friend, and I am one of His many children.

God told Eve not to eat of the tree of the knowledge of good and evil.

She was disobedient so sin and death entered into the world. Thanks be to God for His Son and our Savior the Lord Jesus Christ.

How many people will die today? How many people will die tomorrow?

Did they not want to continue living? Did they not want to see the child at play?

Seek the Lord with all of your heart, soul, mind and strength. Seek the eternal and not the temporal things of the world.

On the day that we die, may we hear well done good and faithful servant from our Lord.

The Lord placed an Omega sign above me a few months ago. The cloud was perfectly designed as the Greek alphabet letter is designed, the sign of the Omega.

Warn your friends to stop living in darkness and pray fervently for them.

It is a joy walking in the power of the Holy Ghost. It is a joy seeking the face of the Almighty.

The children are His hearts concern. The children are the reason for His unfailing faithfulness.

The children are His love, and He is their love.

The newborn child and the one-hundred year old child; the children are His hearts concern.

Obedience to the Gospel of Christ creates faith in the blood of the Lamb. His victory was won at the cross.

Study, pray and fast. Seek the Lord with me for He is good.

How many people will die today? How many people will die tomorrow?

Concentrate on the eternal, and not on the temporal.

Walk in the Spirit, and not in the uncleanness of the flesh.

Prepare yourself as the bride of Christ. Prepare yourself as a son or daughter of the Lord God Almighty.

He is risen, He is coming. Even so, hallelujah, Lord come quickly.

Be ready, for the kingdom of Heaven is at hand.

Study, pray and fast. Serve the Lord with me for He is good.

We are warned! We are warned! We are warned! Spend eternity with the King. Pray, study and fast.

In the name of the
Father, the Son and
the Holy Ghost

Amen and Amen
Copyright © 2008

Lion of Judah is His Name

A prayer of Mark Berryhill

Can you hear the thunder roaring, roaring as a great Lion? Lion of Judah is His name.

The Lion of Judah reigns. In righteousness and in equity the Lion of Judah reigns.

Can you hear the thunder roaring, roaring as a great Lion? Lion of Judah is His name.

The Lion of Judah reigns. In righteousness and in equity, the Lion of Judah reigns.

Can you hear the thunder roaring, roaring as a great Lion? Lion of Judah is His name.

The Lion of Judah reigns. In righteousness and in equity, the Lion of Judah reigns.

Have you looked outside tonight? Have you looked at the beauty and brilliance of stars innumerable?

He calls them by name each night. Have you wondered how He can call the stars by name each night?

Meditate upon the Lord. Consider how great the works of His hands truly are!

The government is carried by His strength, and by His knowledge.

He is faithful to those who trust in Him. He is the giver of all good gifts.

Within the arms He cradles the child. Within His heart, His Son is placed.

He created love. He made life, and He is the light of men.

Before the child cries, He is there. Before the child whimpers, He is there.

He knows all things and He loves you so. He is Father, Son and Holy Ghost.

The children are the delight of His heart. The children cause the joy that keeps Him going.

Father, teach these precious lambs Your Word each day.

Father, we love You! Father, we need You! Father, love these children with all of Your being!

Lord Jesus, thank You for Your victory at the cross. Lord Jesus, thank You for the gift of the child. Lord Jesus, thank You for Your blood.

Holy Ghost, dwell within the hearts and minds of these precious lambs.

Holy Ghost, write Your Great Word in the hearts and minds of these precious lambs.

Holy Ghost, You are a joy and a delight. Holy Ghost, thank You for living within the hearts and minds of God's children.

Before the first whimper, even before the child is delivered from the womb, the Lord was there.

You see my friend and loved one, He is all knowing, all powerful, and as gentle as a lamb.

In His greatness and in His love there is no end. His greatness and His love exceed infinite.

He is the Great I AM. He is the Lord and giver of all good things.

When I see the pain the Lord Jesus suffered at the cross, I inquire of Him, why my Lord?

And He says, no greater love has any man than to lay down His life for the ones He loves.

At the cross was joy and victory. I told you that I love you days and months and years without end He said.

He saw the victory that He won for us because He loved us.

He knew that his Father would raise Him as He will raise us.

You see my children, my handsome son, and my beautiful daughter, faith is increased through the knowledge of His Word.

Lord Jesus, I love You. Lord Jesus, I need You. Lord Jesus, thank You for blessings without end.

Exalt the Lord with me for He is good. His mercy and grace and greatness and love endure forevermore.

My precious children, Jesus is great. My children may He be Your all in all.

Can you hear the thunder roaring, roaring as a great Lion? Lion of Judah is His name.

The Lion of Judah reigns. In righteousness and in equity, the Lion of Judah reigns.

In the name of the
Father, the Son and
the Holy Ghost

Amen and Amen

In the Spirit of Thanksgiving

A song of Mark Berryhill

Father, fill us with the spirit of thanksgiving.

Help us to always see the good and not the bad.

Father, please give us, Your children, the spirit of thanksgiving.

Father, may we become a people filled with the Holy Ghost.
Father, may our lives be ever spent loving, and seeking You.

Father, teach us Your ways. Father, teach us to love You with all of our being.

Lord Jesus, thank You for our children. Lord Jesus, thank You for the blessing of the child.

Father, thank You for carrying all of these lambs by Your strength and by Your love.

So as it is written, love will cover a multitude of sins.

Father, thank You for the magnificent love displayed by You at the cross.

Father, thank You for telling us that You love us more than You love Yourself.

Lord Jesus, thank You from all of us that can see the pain and agony You suffered at the cross.

Lord Jesus, thank You for buying us at the cross. Help us to be as faithful to You as You were to Your Father.

Within the heart of God's child dwells Father, Son and Holy Ghost.

How important is the intent of the heart? Is the motive of the heart to be weighed by the Father?

How important is the intent of the heart? Is the motive of the heart to be weighed by the Father?

Tell me if you can, how important is the intent of the heart? Is the motive of the heart to be weighed by the Father?

With blood dripping down from the thorns in His innocent head, tell me if you can the motive of your Father.

With tears of pain flowing down His precious cheeks, my friend, can you tell me the motive of His heart?

My friends weigh the motive of His heart if you can.

I love you He said, and I love you with all that I AM!

In the name of the
Father, the Son and
the Holy Ghost

Amen and Amen
Copyright © 2008

This is Holy Ground

A prayer of Mark Berryhill

When you look across this great land, what do you see?

When you look across this great land, what do you want to see?

May we see the children, both young and old meditating on God's Word as were His servants of old.

Knowledge is from the Lord. Love and happiness are from the Lord.

My friends, my loved ones, diligently seek the face of our King.

Love Him, and serve Him with study, prayer and fasting.

Knowledge of the holy comes from the Holy One, for He is the Holy One of Israel.

May we see the children both young and old meditating on God's Word as were His servants of old.

Consider the beauty of God's universe.

Consider the baby birds that are safely residing in their nests.

Consider the fawn as she prances eloquently through the open field.

Consider the beauty of untouched trees that reach into the Heavens.

Consider the black bear that is walking ever so closely to the water of the lake.

He is hungry and his prey is near.

Consider the pike and wall-eye fish that were so properly prepared for the feast.

Consider the beauty of the sound of the wind as it gently glides through untouched trees and then returns from where He came.

Consider the majesty of snow capped mountains throughout the earth.

Consider the beauty of roaming deserts that stretch endlessly throughout this great land.

Have you considered that God feeds the animals that call these deserts their home each day?

Consider life and then consider death. Consider the horror of eternal separation and eternal damnation separated from our Father.

Consider the everlasting beauty of eternal life in paradise with our Father.

Learn the Word, live the Word and teach the Word. Walk in the light as He is in the light.

Exalt the Lord with me all of you saints, for He is good.

In the name of the
Father, the Son and
the Holy Ghost

Amen and Amen
Copyright © 2008

Thank Him for His Grace and Mercy

A song of Mark Berryhill

Have you ever noticed how beautiful the plants, trees and grass become following an abundance of rain?

Have you ever noticed how desolate and unattractive plants, trees and grass become without rain?

Throughout the writings of the Holy Scriptures, God has blessed His children with rain for obedience, and has withheld rain for disobedience.

Our bodies are the temple of the true and living God.

We must care for and nurture our bodies as what they truly are, the Temple of the true and living God.

Drink an abundance of water, and eat healthy.

Not as a commandment but as a blessing for each one of us; let us eat bountifully the fruits, vegetables and soups that the Lord so graciously provides.

Fasting has been one of the most overlooked blessings of recent years.

Fasting is an act of worship to the Lord, teaches us discipline and keeps us healthier.

As the blood of our Savior is our eternal life, so the blood within our bodies is our temporal life. Let us do all that we can to keep our blood pure and clean.

Knowledge is more readily acquired provided a person fasts regularly, and memory retention capability increases substantially.

Study diligently, pray without ceasing and fast regularly and often.

Drink an abundance of water, and completely abstain from alcohol and the unhealthy drinks.

Love the LORD your God with all of your heart, with all of your soul, with all of your mind and with all of your strength. Love your neighbor as yourself.

Keep the vows of marriage. Be holy and faithful to your spouse.

If you are an unmarried child of God, remember that you are the bride of Christ and that sexual purity is a commandment, and not a choice.

The Lord desires to bless His children. Knowledge and wisdom are found only in the Holy Scriptures.

My blessed child is it true that the Lord reveals His secrets to His servants the prophets?

He says that He is the same yesterday, today and forever.

His love for His children reaches higher than the highest star of the Heaven of Heavens.

With grace and mercy that endures throughout infinity, He will write His Word on the hearts and minds of His children Israel.

In the name of the
Father, the Son and
the Holy Ghost

Amen and Amen
Copyright © 2008

The Beauty is His Son

A song of Mark Berryhill

Hand you ever noticed how beautiful the plants, trees and grass become following an abundance of rain?

Have you ever noticed how desolate and unattractive plants, trees and grass become without rain?

Throughout the writings of the Holy Scriptures, God has blessed His children with rain for obedience, and has withheld rain for disobedience.

Our bodies are the temple of the true and living God.

We must care for and nurture our bodies as what they truly are, the Temple of the true and living God.

Drink an abundance of water, and eat healthy.

Not as a commandment but as a blessing for each one of us; let us eat bountifully the fruits, vegetables and soups that the Lord so graciously provides.

Fasting has been one of the most overlooked blessings of recent years.

Fasting is an act of worship to the Lord, teaches us discipline and keeps us healthier.

As the blood of our Savior is our eternal life, so the blood within our bodies is our temporal life. Let us do all that we can to keep our blood pure and clean.

Knowledge is more readily acquired provided a person fasts regularly, and memory retention capability increases substantially.

Study diligently, pray without ceasing and fast regularly and often.

Drink and abundance of water, and completely abstain from alcohol and the unhealthy drinks.

Love the LORD your God with all of your heart, with all of your soul, with all of your mind and with all of your strength. Love your neighbor as yourself.

Keep the vows of marriage. Be holy and faithful to your spouse.

If you are an unmarried child of God, remember that you are the bride of Christ and that sexual purity is a commandment, and not a choice.

The Lord desires to bless His children. Knowledge and wisdom are found only in the Holy Scriptures.

My blessed child is it true that the Lord reveals His secrets to His servants the prophets?

He says that He is the same yesterday, today and forever.

His love for His children reaches higher than the highest star of the Heaven of Heavens.

With grace and mercy that endures throughout infinity, He will writes His Word on the hearts and minds of His children Israel.

In the name of the
Father, the Son and
the Holy Ghost

Amen and Amen
Copyright © 2008

The Beauty is His Son

A song of Mark Berryhill

Dwell in the light of the Lord. Dwell in the light with the Lord.
Father, teach us to be perfect in both flesh and spirit.

Train us as You trained our Savior the Lord Jesus.

Teach us how to discern good and evil as you discern good and evil.

May we care for and love the fatherless, and widows in their affliction as You care for and love the fatherless and widows in their affliction.

As You trained Jesus, may You and Jesus train us in the world of spirits.

Father, fill us with the Holy Ghost. As on the day of Pentecost may You pour Him upon and within us.

Baptism into Jesus is the light of walking in obedience to commandment.

Lord Jesus, we praise You this day. Lord Jesus, we love You this day.

Lord Jesus, thank You for the beauty of this creation. Lord Jesus, thank You for the beauty of life.

Lord Jesus, thank You for eternal life. Lord Jesus, thank You for Your victory at the cross.

Father, thank You for the gift of fasting. Thank You for the magnificence of Your power residing so readily.

Lord, teach us how to study Your Word while we study.

We pray for knowledge and understanding from You.

We exalt You today because we love You.

Father, thank You for the beauty of the birth of newborn children.

The birth of a newborn child is without question one of Your greatest gifts to Your people.

You my Lord are an awesome God. You my Lord are our great reward.

Father, teach us to enjoy the beauty of Your creation. Teach us to rest in Your love for each one of us.

May I see the cross of Your Son always before me. May the picture of Your precious Son be ever present before my spiritual eyes.

Orange, violet, white, light blue, light green and dark green are beautiful colors my Lord and my God.

Holy Ghost, have we told You that we love You today?

Lord Jesus, have we told You that we need You this day?

Father, have we told You that we thank You and praise You for the blood of the Lamb?

Eternal One. Eternal victory. Jesus won the race on the tree at Calvary.

He is risen and He is coming. Even so Lord Jesus come quickly.

May the grace of our Lord Jesus Christ be with you all.

In the name of the
Father, the Son and
the Holy Ghost

Amen and Amen
Copyright © 2008

Speaking in Tongues

A song Mark Berryhill

The Lord just blessed me with my first experience of speaking in tongues.

The experience was exhilarating.

Study, prayer and diligent fasting have a direct correlation to this wonderful experience. His awesome presence, power and peace become so evident.

The Lord is a rewarder of good things to those who diligently seek Him.

Father, Lord Jesus, Holy Ghost, thank You for the unexpected gift of speaking in tongues.

Glorify God with speaking in tongues. Take off your shoes, lift up holy hands high to the sky and pray.

Love Him and serve Him for days without end.

In the name of the
Father, the Son and
the Holy Ghost

Amen and Amen
Copyright © 2008

Mercy and Love

A prayer of Mark Berryhill

Holy, Holy, Holy Lord God Almighty, which was, and is and is to come.

Exalt the Lord with me for He is good. His mercy, grace and love will never end.

Can you fathom what it must be like to be the Father of all?

Can you fathom what it must be like to know all things simultaneously?

Why would He take of His time to show you how much that He loves you?

Why would He create creatures in His own image? Why would He create creatures in the likeness of Him?

I ask You Lord, why do You create these precious and fragile babies.

Because I AM.

Father, thank You for the gift of Your Son. Thank You for the victory of the cross.

Jesus, I love You! Jesus, I need You! Jesus, I adore You!

Exalt the Lord with me for He is good. His mercy, grace and love will never end.

How much do you love your son? How much do you love your daughter?

The love that you have for your son and daughter is nothing compared to the love the Holy Ghost has for you.

He is all powerful. He is all knowing. He is the love of mankind.

The Holy Ghost is our Divine guide. He is from the Father of lights.

His mercy, grace and love will never end.

He is Father, Son and Holy Ghost.

Which of these do you consider the greatest: faith, hope or charity?

May our Father bless us with faith, as the Blessed Trinity's faith.

May our Father, the rewarder of good things to those who diligently seek Him, bless us with hope as the Blessed Trinity's hope.

May our Father, the giver of all good gifts bless us with charity as the Blessed Trinity's charity.

In the name of the
Father, the Son and
the Holy Ghost

Amen and Amen
Copyright © 2008

He is the Great I AM

A prayer of Mark Berryhill

Who is the Holy Ghost? What does He do for me? Why would I want or need a Ghost dwelling within my heart?

He is the light of the heart! He is the guide within the children of Jesus Christ.

Why is He so important? He is important because He, as the Father and Son, can do all things.

With the Holy Ghost, you my precious child can do all things.

With His strength and with His faith and with His power, you, my precious child can set the world on fire for the King of kings.

He as the Father and as the Son can do all things. Nothing is impossible for the Holy Ghost!

He as the Father and as the Son loves and laughs and cries.

He has a heart of pure love. He has a heart that will become the way of the world.

The Holy Ghost is your friend and He will become even closer to each child of Jesus Christ.

He is faithful and He is the Spirit of truth.

He is the light of mankind. He is to be praised and exalted as the Father and the Son are to be praised and exalted.

With love that reaches from earth to the Heaven of heavens, and with mercy that will exceed infinity, He is the great I AM, Father, Son and Holy Ghost.

In the name of the
Father, the Son and
the Holy Ghost

Amen and Amen
Copyright © 2008

Praise God for His Lamb

A prayer of Mark Berryhill

The man I visited with this morning is skin and bones. From his appearance he seemed as a weak man.

But there was no fear in the eyes of the man who appeared as a weak man.

He is a man of faith. He is a man of God. In his Lord he fully trusts.

I had told him before that it is the weak and feeble who are often times most needed.

Why would that be so? The fervent prayers of righteous men and women availeth much says the Lord God of Israel.

As we become weak, He becomes strong. As our fleshly bodies are deteriorating day by day, our spirit is being renewed and strengthened by the power of the Holy Ghost day by day.

Life suddenly becomes worth living for the dying when this simple truth becomes reality.

All praise, glory and honor unto the Father, the Son and the Holy Ghost.

Hallelujah for His Lamb! Hallelujah for His Lamb! Hallelujah for His Lamb!

As Zephaniah wrote, "The Lord thy God in the midst of thee is mighty; He will save, He will rejoice over thee with joy; He will rest in His love, He will joy over thee with singing."[12]

Jesus we will set Your name on high. We will love You with all of our hearts, souls, minds and strength.

Holy, holy, holy Lord God Almighty, which was, and is and is to come.

---

[12] King James Version Zephaniah 3:17

We will walk and live from this day forward in the power of the Holy Ghost.

The weak man is becoming a strong man. The weak man belongs to the King of kings.

In the name of the
Father, the Son and
the Holy Ghost

Amen and Amen
Copyright © 2008

I AM THAT I AM

A prayer of Mark Berryhill

How important is the time a father spends with his son and daughter?

How important is the time that You spend with us Almighty Father?

Father, Son and Holy Ghost, thank You for the gift of the child. Thank You for the gift and relationship between us and You and the relationship between fathers and their children throughout this blessed earth.

Father, I love You! Jesus, I need You! Spirit, we adore You!

Love us and mold us with Your skillful hands.

Lord God, what will Heaven be like? How beautiful is the Heaven of heavens?

My Lord, these precious children need to be nurtured with Your love, and with Your guidance.

Love them, cherish them, nurture them and lead them by the power of the Holy Ghost!

He is Father. He is Son. He is Holy Ghost. He is I AM THAT I AM.

Can you hear the laughter of the child at play? Can you see the beauty of children residing safely in the bosom of the Father?

He is the great I AM!

He is Father, Son and Holy Ghost.

Can you see the love that resides within His heart? Can you hear Him as He sings over you with joy in His heart this very night?

He is my Father. He is my Savior. He is the Spirit that resides within His children.

Father, You are an awesome God indeed. Lord Jesus, You are an awesome Lord indeed. Holy Ghost, You have become our joy and delight.

Did you know that He loves, laughs and cries? You see my friend; He created us, His called-out children in His image and in His likeness.

How great is the Father who created life? What is His name? What is His Son's name?

How great is the blood of the Lamb? Eternal One. Eternal love. Eternal victory. Jesus Christ is His name.

In the name of the
Father, the Son and
the Holy Ghost

Amen and Amen
Copyright © 2008

Victor of Eternal Life

A song of Mark Berryhill

The grass and trees are manicured with perfection in mind. The old building is well maintained and nicely painted.

Actually the eloquence of the building is vivid and the peace of the Lord rests upon the beautiful people that are in attendance this particular morning.

Within the building the priest excitedly and confidently leads prayers, songs and Bible lessons.

Hallelujah he proclaims all praise, glory and honor to the Father, the Son and the Holy Ghost.

The choir begins harmonizing wonderfully and the presence of the Holy Spirit becomes even more real as the other people join in with the choir in singing.

The guitarist soon afterward joins in and adds even more beauty to the picturesque scene.

The people are there for one reason. The people are there to serve the Creator of life and Victor of eternal life.

The people are exalting the Lord in word and in deed.

The people are helping Father, Son and Holy Ghost feed His lambs.

The lambs of Jesus Christ are His reason for existence. To feed the lambs of Father, Son and Holy Ghost is the reason for life.

Do you love the Father? Feed His lambs. Do you love the Son? Feed His lambs. Do you love the Holy Spirit? Feed His lambs.

The elderly man walked with a severe limp. As he was leaving the building he stopped briefly to visit with the priest.

The priest greeted him with a greeting of joy, reverence and eloquence.

The Spirit of love and the Spirit of humility rest upon the man of

God. The elderly man departed from church that morning walking in the newness of life.

The elderly man is a lamb of God.

In the name of the
Father, the Son and
the Holy Ghost

Amen and Amen
Copyright © 2008

He is a Gracious LORD

A song of Mark Berryhill

Last year the man said to trust in yourself. He was confident that he was responsible for his success.

Today the same man is attentive to the calling of His Creator the Almighty God.

The man for too many years enjoyed the alcohol that has silently destroyed his liver.

The Lord, being gracious to him, is giving him time to learn about the Lord Jesus Christ.

Last year another man that had helped me too many times to write about, passed away with cancer.

The man was my dad. I loved him so. For years I had asked my precious dad to put away the tobacco that he craved as I had once craved it.

Your body and my body are the tabernacles of the living God.

Keep your spirit and body pure. Avoid and denounce all of the temptations that are put in front of you.

There is a man that is a preacher. The man is a man of God.

My father, who I loved so, told me that the man of God begins each morning by arising at four in the morning.

When there is a place for him to swim, I understand that he begins his morning at that time by swimming.

After that exercise his meditation on the Lord begins. He is a diligent studier of the only book in the world that we truly need.

He is a preacher of the good news of the gospel of Jesus Christ.

How many souls has the Lord used the preacher to save?

Keep yourself pure. Father, we pray that You will help us to keep ourselves perfect in both body and spirit.

Father, we love You! Jesus, we need You! Spirit, we adore You!
Lead us in all that we do!

In the name of the
Father, the Son and
the Holy Ghost

Amen and Amen

Love, Faith and Hope

A prayer of Mark Berryhill

For a few moments Father and Son were separated.

The tears were flowing freely down the precious cheeks of Immanuel.

Were they tears of sadness or were they tears of joy?

My friends tell me if you can, were Immanuel's tears tear's of sadness or tears of joy?

The Father is Son. The Father is Holy Ghost.

Who felt more pain on the day of Calvary, Father, Son or Holy Ghost?

Wise men, wise woman tell me if you can who felt more pain on the day of Calvary, Father, Son or Holy Ghost?

On the day of Calvary, who experienced more joy, Father, Son or Holy Ghost?

Wise friend, on the day of Calvary, who experienced more joy, Father, Son or Holy Ghost?

Father, Son and Holy Ghost have become our lives. Thank You for Your creation and for your brilliant plan of salvation.

He cried My child, where are you? Can you see beloved child that it was the Father crying on the day of Calvary?

With unseen tears flowing down our invisible Father's face, it was the Father of all who felt the pain of Calvary.

I asked my Father how much He loves each child. He answered by saying, will you allow your child to die for the sins of these people?

Lord Jesus, thank You for Your victory at the cross of Calvary!

Father, Son and Holy Ghost are the Blessed Trinity. He is Creator, Sustainer, Savior and friend of the child.

He is I AM THAT I AM. Wise man, wise woman remember that He created the child.

In reference to love, faith and hope: love is the greatest of these.

In the name of the
Father, the Son and
the Holy Ghost

Amen and Amen

The Beauty of God's Child

A prayer of Mark Berryhill

He is risen. He is coming. Even so Lord Jesus, come quickly. Amen.

In life obstacles and struggles become blessings and opportunities.

He formed you in the womb of your mother. He breathed life into Adam and he became a living soul.

He spoke and light came into existence. He is the great I AM.

He has a heart of pure love and this morning He heard His child say the Pledge of Allegiance.

His heart was touched and today His excitement for living is renewed.

He became wise because He is the Word. He became flesh so that He could give His life a ransom for many.

He is Father, Son and Holy Ghost.

The fear of the Lord is pure and clean. Father help me and these precious children to fear you all of our days.

He became wise because He meditated on the Word day and night.

He gave us the free gift of His child. We are a blessed and loved people.

My precious son and my precious daughter, Jesus loves you so. Write His Word on the table of your hearts.

In the name of the
Father, the Son and
the Holy Ghost

Amen and Amen
Copyright © 2008

Jesus Christ: the Power of God and the Wisdom of God

A prayer of Mark Berryhill

He was left alone by those whom had told Him that they loved Him. As the fire of persecution arose, they withered from the heat. They had slept while He had prayed. Thank You for the avenue of prayer Lord Jesus. Thank You for the free and undeserved gift of Your child Almighty Father.

The innocent man hung on the tree in order to set you free from the guilt and worry of sins that were nailed with Him at the cross on the day of Calvary.

That day Jesus said that I love you. My Father knows all things. Walk with Me in the light today and henceforth He says.

Most of the same men who had withered from the heat of the fire of persecution earlier, later gave their lives for the ones whom they had said they loved. They had understood what Jesus meant when He said, "greater love hath no man than this, that a man lay down his life for his friends."[13]

Father God, help us feed Your precious lambs Your Word today and each day henceforth. Father, how great You are! Jesus, how great You are! Holy Ghost, how great You are!

Father, thank You for Jesus. Father, thank You for the eternal power of the blood of Your lamb. Thank You for the gift of the Holy Ghost.

In the name of the
Father, the Son and
the Holy Ghost

Amen and Amen
Copyright © 2008

---

[13] King James Version John 15:13

His Greatest Treasure

A song of Mark Berryhill

I was praying and asking the Lord to reveal a new message to me.

While considering what I had asked for He revealed to me the greatest treasure of life.

A few short hours before, I had met a precious little boy who I suppose was about three or maybe four years old.

The Lord said there is your revelation. There is the greatest treasure ever created by the Father of lights.

The greatest treasure in the world is the child. Whether boy or girl is irrelevant. His love for them is the same.

He can do all things. He was, He is and He is to be.

Knowledge, understanding, wisdom and revelation come forth from the book known by one of His many names, THE WORD OF GOD.

Have you ever noticed that every move of a child expresses their excitement and joy for life.

Their excitement and joy for life is another of God's many treasures.

Father, I had once said that ten more children for me would do my Lord.

However, after considering more diligently Lord Jesus, I suppose that eleven more will be even better.

Enjoy life. Enjoy the treasures that God so bountifully and magnificently bestows upon His children.

He is all knowing. He is all powerful. He is a Father, Son and Spirit that have placed their children in their heart.

He created life. He created the child. He created everything beautiful.

He is the Holy One of Israel. He was, He is and is to be.
Love Him with all of your heart, soul, mind and strength.
Let us make Him our only reason for living.

In the name of the
Father, the Son and
the Holy Ghost

Amen and Amen

Enjoy the Beauty of Life

A song of Mark Berryhill

The mother says that she loves her children but she will not take the necessary time that is required to feed her children God's Word.

Obedience brings rewards and blessings while disobedience brings punishment.

I pray Lord God that You will deliver the children into my hands and watch me raise them in the daily admonition and nurture of the Lord.

Thank You for all the rain Lord Jesus.

The air is so fresh and clean. The varied colors of the sky are very pleasant to the eyes today.

Lord Jesus, thank You for the grass which has become so beautiful and green because of all of the rain.

Thank You for the pretty tall trees that the birds rest in and call their home.

Thank You for the beauty and life each plant brings into our lives.

The land that had become a dry and barren land quickly became a land filled with an abundance of rain.

Obedience to the Gospel of Jesus Christ brings showers of blessings while disobedience will bring His wrath and destruction.

Father may we learn to fear You as Jesus fears You.

Father may we learn to love You as Jesus loves You.

Father may we learn to trust You as Jesus trusts You.

Father, Son and Holy Ghost. Who was, and is and is to come.

Blessed be Father, Son and Holy Ghost; one and the same.

In the name of the
Father, the Son and
the Holy Ghost

Amen and Amen
Copyright © 2008

Each Season is for Praising the Holy Ghost

A song of Mark Berryhill

Who is the Holy Ghost? Does He love me? Should I serve Him?

The Holy Ghost is one of the Blessed Trinity. As the Father and Son are to be loved and worshipped, so is the Holy Ghost to be loved and worshipped.

He is the Spirit of the true and living God. As the Father and Son can do all things, so also can the Holy Ghost do all things.

There is nothing that is impossible for Him. He was, He is and He is to come!

He is the light and guide of Jesus Christ's children. He is to be loved, worshipped and obeyed as the Father and as the Son are to be worshipped and obeyed.

He is the Spirit of truth and He is the Comforter. He lives and dwells within the hearts and minds of God's chosen and called-out children.

He is Father, Son and Holy Ghost.

In the name of the
Father, the Son and
the Holy Ghost

Amen and Amen
Copyright © 2008

Be Ever Present Lord Jesus

A prayer of Mark Berryhill

May Your face be ever present before me Lord Jesus.

May I see You at all times and may you be ever present within the hearts of my children.

May they also see Your face before them at all times.

Today has been another blessed day. Today was another day to seek and serve the King of kings.

Father fill these precious children with Your Word. Help them and myself to meditate on Your Word day and night without ceasing.

Father we need to have a revival for You. We want to sing and dance before You with all of our might.

Father thank You for the rain today. Father thank You for the gift of another day.

Thank You for the gift of life Lord Jesus. More importantly, thank You for the gift of eternal life.

Thank You for Your victory at the cross.

Holy Ghost, I pray that You will open the doors so that we can serve You, Jesus and our Father all day every day.

In the name of the
Father, the Son and
the Holy Ghost

Amen and Amen
Copyright © 2008

Eternal Inheritance: Jesus Christ is His Name

A prayer of Mark Berryhill

Train us in the Spirit Lord Jesus.
Teach us to be perfect in both the flesh and spirit.
Moral purity is a commandment, not a choice.
Consider how much you love your son and your daughter.
Christ's love for you is even greater than the love you have for your own son and daughter.
Eternal inheritance. Jesus Christ is His name.

In the name of the
Father, the Son and
the Holy Ghost

Amen and Amen
Copyright © 2008

In His Word is Knowledge, Wisdom and Understanding

A prayer of Mark Berryhill

Father we need for You to become more prevalent in our daily lives.

We need You to stay closer to us.

Father thank You for today. Help me to meditate on Your Word day and night.

Father thank You for Your Word. Thank You for Jesus and His blood.

Father we exalt You today because we love You!

Lord Jesus we exalt You today because we love You!

When the child needed to be fed the Word, did You feed the child the Word?

When the spirit of the child craved knowledge, wisdom and understanding, did you feed the child's spirit with His Father's Word?

Concentrate on the eternal and not on the temporal.

The temporal things of this world will pass away. Jesus Christ will endure forevermore.

Meditate on God's Word day and night. Let His Word become your heart and mind.

The Father, the Son and the Holy Ghost are eternal. Spend eternity with them in paradise.

Teach us Your Word Almighty Father.

In the name of the
Father, the Son and
the Holy Ghost

Amen and Amen
Copyright © 2008

Brilliantly Created by You

A prayer of Mark Berryhill

The Holy Ghost is the light of man. He carries God's children through this exciting adventure known to man as life.

He is to be exalted and loved as the Father and the Son are exalted and loved. He is the Comforter. He is the Spirit of truth.

Holy Ghost, thank You for leading the hearts and minds of God's called-out children.

Father, You say that to keep Your commandments is to love You. I am walking in the light because I love You and I fear You so.

Father, how can I show You how much I love You? Feed the lamb's every day. Make every day a day set apart for Me He said.

Father, don't forget to stop and enjoy the fragrance of beautiful roses brilliantly created by You.

White, yellow, burgundy, pink and violet are such beautiful colors Almighty Father.

Father open Your heart and love these children. Tell them that they are important to You.

Tell them that You are their love, their life and their all in all.

Father, thank You for the time and effort it took You, Jesus and the Holy Spirit to write Your Word.

Father come and heal this great land. Lord Jesus come and heal this great land. Holy Ghost come and heal this great land.

My friend, can you tell me how great is the blood of the lamb?

How great is the eternal power of the blood of God's Lamb?

Eternal One. Eternal victory. Jesus Christ is His name.

Father remember to stop and enjoy the fragrance of beautiful roses brilliantly created by You.

Father remember to stop and enjoy the beauty of the smile of a baby boy brilliantly created by You.

111

Father remember to stop and enjoy the beauty of the smile of a baby girl brilliantly created by You.

Father You are the brilliant One. Eternal One. Eternal Victory. Jesus Christ is His name.

Father, Son and Holy Ghost; Creator of life, Sustainer of life and Victor of eternal life.

Walk in the light as He is in the light.

In the name of the
Father, the Son and
the Holy Ghost

Amen and Amen
Copyright © 2008

He Touched my Heart

A song of Mark Berryhill

She is beautiful. She brings love, joy and happiness to all who know her.

She is a daughter of the Most High.

This particular evening she was being very unlike herself. She was behaving very rudely.

I had already spanked her once but was going to have to spank her again.

It was then that he touched my heart. My son Nathan asked for me not to spank his sister but to spank him instead. I responded by saying that it was Evan who was misbehaving.

With tears beginning to run down his cheeks and the sobbing becoming louder and louder, it was then that he touched my heart.

He had done no wrong but was willing to take the punishment for wrongs committed by his younger sister. Seeing the beauty of his love so openly displayed toward his sister touched my heart, and eyes of new perspective were opened.

He went to the cross of Calvary because His love for you and me was greater than His love for Himself.

In the name of the
Father, the Son and
the Holy Ghost

Amen and Amen
Copyright © 2008

113

A Heart as the Heart of Christ's Heart

A song of Mark Berryhill

Nighttime is unquestionably one of God's greatest blessings to mankind. It is during the night that God reveals himself to us through the brilliance of shining stars.

This morning while I was working on cutting my second lawn of the day I saw a picture that will move the world a little bit closer to Christ.

There was a young boy so happy that I was caring for his family's lawn. We have had almost three weeks of rain and the grass was extremely tall.

The young boy was so excited about being able to help me by moving some small rocks and paper that were in the way of mowing.

The Lord revealed two pictures to me on this particular morning.

First, each one of us need to be moving about our Father's work as excitedly as the young boy was about helping me.

Secondly, we need the spirit of obedience residing in us as it was so evidently demonstrated in the boy this particular morning.

Father give us a heart that is open and attentive to Your holy commandments.

Father give us the spirit of obedience that was so beautifully demonstrated this morning by the precious young boy.

Father give us a heart as the heart of Christ's heart.

In the name of the
Father, the Son and
the Holy Ghost

Amen and Amen
Copyright © 2008

God of Love, Faith and Hope

A prayer of Mark Berryhill

With hands firmly placed together in the Heaven of heavens He prays without ceasing.

As He prays without ceasing so also should we be praying without ceasing.

Study and meditate on the Holy Scriptures. Let the Word of God become you.

Let the Word of God become your reason for living.

Share the gospel of Jesus Christ with others. Share the good news of the gospel of God's Son.

Time is a precious commodity. Spend the time the Lord gives you wisely meditating in His Word.

Study and see why His words make life worth living.

In the name of the
Father, the Son and
the Holy Ghost

Amen and Amen
Copyright © 2008

Words of Eternal Life

A song of Mark Berryhill

The prayer that will move the people of God just a little bit closer to the Father.

Time is and always has been one of mankind's most precious commodities.

Within the scope of time a man and a woman become what their Creator created them to become.

For our thoughts to be pure and kept pure we must be concentrating on and memorizing the Holy Scriptures.

Our Father has taken several thousand years to write the greatest book that has ever been written or ever will be written.

His Word is truth. His Word is living and within His Word are the words of eternal life.

Each of us will give an account for our actions to Jesus Christ.

May our actions be motivated by pure hearts which extend love to our Father and for our fellow man.

Holy Ghost please teach us how to study. Please teach us what to study.

Holy Ghost give us knowledge and wisdom in the management of our time.

My precious son and my beautiful daughter begin your walk with your Father while you are young.

Let every thought that we have be brought into the captivity of obedience to our Lord Jesus.

Begin memorizing the Holy Scriptures while you are young and tender so that when you are old and feeble you will know how strong and powerful your Father truly is.

His name is Father, Son and Holy Ghost. He is unchanging. He is the same yesterday, today and forever.

As He dwells in an unapproachable light so shall we walk in the light of Christ from this day and henceforth.

In the name of the
Father, the Son and
the Holy Ghost

Amen and Amen

Being Supreme

A song of Mark Berryhill

He is holy. We are to be a holy People.

He is the light of man. He is the giver of all good things.

Life is precious. Life is short. As He is in the light, let us walk in the light from this day and henceforth.

He won the victory at the cross. He suffered pain for you and me because He loves us with all of His Being.

He is the Supreme Being. He was before the light and will remain infinitely.

At the cross He said, I love you with all that I AM!

In the name of the
Father, the Son and
the Holy Ghost

Amen and Amen
Copyright © 2008

His Love for the Child

A song of Mark Berryhill

When all is said and done and He asks each one of us what we accomplished for Him. May we be able to look into His eyes and say for You Lord Jesus we gave our all.

May His response be as music dancing in our ears. I know You gave your all for Me, well done good and faithful servant.

In the world of the Spirit sadness becomes joy, pain becomes comfort and sickness becomes wholeness.

He is a God who is perfect. He is a God that spoke and light came into existence.

While you sleep He stands beside you and watches over you. While you work and play He walks beside you for no other reason except that He loves you.

He lives within His called-out children and He walks beside us on this short journey here on earth we call life.

He is all powerful. He is all knowing. He is the Almighty.

His love for the child is shown beautifully and perfectly by His infinite victory known as the Cross of Calvary.

In the name of the
Father, the Son and
the Holy Ghost

Amen and Amen
Copyright © 2008

By God's Right Hand

A song of Mark Berryhill

Father, guide my every thought with Your Spirit.
Father, guide the children's hearts with Your Spirit.
Tell them that You love them Lord Jesus.
Knock on their door so they will know that You care.
His hand reached out from Heaven. His hand reached out and told us that He loved us.
His hand placed His well beloved on the cross.
You see my friend, at the cross Jesus won the victory of eternal life for His children.
My friends and my loved ones, walk in the light as He is in the light.
Stay pure in the Spirit and in the flesh.
Meditate on the Lord. Meditate on His Word.
Pray without ceasing unto the giver of all good things.
Thank Him for His Son and for their victory at the cross of Calvary.

In the name of the
Father, the Son and
the Holy Ghost

Amen and Amen
Copyright © 2008

Heart of Jehovah

A song of Mark Berryhill

Can the heart of Jehovah be mended after being broken?

Can His smile ever return to its former glory?

Can His daughter, the very reason for existence, change her life of sin to a life of beauty?

Can His daughter not hear the gentle whisper of His voice saying, I love you with all that I AM!

Can His daughter not understand the pathway of righteousness ordained for her before the Heavens were spread forth or the foundations of the earth laid?

Can she not hear the gentle whisper of the Great I AM, I love you with all that I AM!

In the name of the
Father, the Son and
the Holy Ghost

Amen and Amen
Copyright © 2008

Who is the Holy Ghost?

A song of Mark Berryhill

Do you love the Holy Ghost? Who is He? Why should I love Him?

He is the Comforter and the Spirit of truth. He is God's invisible guide for us who love the Lord and want to serve Him with all of our being.

The Holy Ghost guides us to God's truth. He teaches us how God would have us to live during this short journey here on earth called life.

He is also the Spirit which makes up what is known as the Blessed Trinity.

He will not only lead you to the truth of God's Word, but He will also teach you how to pray and how to study.

He is alive and He is on fire for JESUS! He is more real than either you or I and He loves you with all of His heart, with all of His soul, with all of His mind, and with all of His strength.

All praise, glory and honor to God the Father, the Lord Jesus Christ and the Holy Ghost. Let us exalt the Blessed Trinity every day. He is Creator, Savior and Guide of God's called-out children.

Shortly after our Lord Jesus had been crucified and the people had began to realize that they had indeed crucified God's true Son, they asked Peter what they should do and Peter preached one of the greatest sermons ever recorded. "Then Peter said unto them, repent and be baptized every one of you in the name of Jesus Christ for remission of sins, and ye shall receive the gift of the Holy Ghost. For the promise is unto You, and to Your children, and to all that are afar off, even as many as the Lord our God shall call."[14]

Who are You Father, Son and Holy Ghost? A still small voice replies, I AM THAT I AM.

---

[14] King James Version Acts 2:38

And I quote I John 1:7, "but if we walk in the light, as He is in the light, we have fellowship one with another, and the blood of Jesus Christ His Son cleanseth us from all sin."[15]

We love You, Father, Son and Holy Ghost!

In the name of the
Father, the Son and
the Holy Ghost

Amen and Amen
Copyright © 2008

---

[15] King James Version I John 1:7

The Beauty of the Cross

A song of Mark Berryhill

The light reflects off of the gentle moving waves of the lake and creates a picturesque scene of tranquility.

As the brilliant bright orange sun begins its decent for the evening, one can see that the Creator of the beauty of the universe and of life is the true artist.

The sun is slowly transformed into a soft color of pink and the clouds appear to come to life. It is as though they also are singing and rejoicing over the beauty of God's majestic and overwhelming creation.

Why did He take the time to create you? Why does He love you with all of His heart, soul, mind and strength?

I suppose that He loves you with all that He is because He formed you with His delicate fingers in the womb of your mother.

The great mountains that reach into the Heavens cry out and say, worship God for He is the great I AM!

Rejoice and be glad for your Father is singing and dancing with joy in His heart over you at this very moment.

Listen to the great seas which roar because of the wind commanded by His voice and by His strength. His clouds readily bring forth His rain for an obedient people who love and serve Him with all of their being.

He is God. He is the provider of the life, light and love of mankind. We, His called-out children learn to truly love Him, and to truly trust in Him as He walks and talks with us through His Word.

He turns tears of sadness into tears of joy. He turns cries of pain and agony into cries of laughter and rejoicing. He turns children of darkness into children of light.

As though by a stroke of a pen JEHOVAH signed the victory which is known as the cross of His Son Jesus Christ.

He is my provision. He is my life and He will become yours if you want a Father who will never leave you nor forsake you.

In the name of the
Father, the Son and
the Holy Ghost

Amen and Amen

Christ's Goal for the Child

A prayer of Mark Berryhill

The child brings such joy into the heart of the Father. Indeed as a closer look is taken, the child remembers the Father so evermore closely.

He is indeed young and tender. Can't you see that he was created in the image and likeness of His Creator? He loves his mother and her family as I suppose his Father God loves him.

He knows at the early age of eight that His Father is the Lord God Almighty. He is quickly becoming a young man.

The formative years of the child are so important to his physical and spiritual well being. The formative years are before his conception until his death.

He must be taught his Father's Word each day. I know that His Father will teach him how to truly study the greatest book ever written.

From before conception until after death may the child be ever hearing The Word of His Father. From the time the child can read until the time God takes him home, may he be meditating on the Lord and on His Word.

Power, knowledge, wisdom and understanding also comedown from the Father of lights. The Lord hears our every thought and He knows our every move.

May our every thought and every move be about Him and about glorifying Him.

Are knowledge and wisdom truly worth more than silver and gold? Jesus Christ is the truth and He is eternal.

My son, my precious gift from God, spend your life serving your Father, the Lord God Almighty. He and His Son are eternal life.

The temporal pleasures of the world only bring sin and death into one's life.

The heart of the child is to be more valued than silver or gold. For the heart of the child is delicately and wonderfully formed by a potter who knows the clay.

The heart of the child is to be protected and guarded against evil by the Holy Scriptures known as the Word of God.

The Father's great book can teach a simple, precious, adorable child that he is a temporal and an eternal being.

Eternal paradise is Christ's goal for the child.

In the name of the
Father, the Son and
the Holy Ghost

Amen and Amen
Copyright © 2008

Delicately and Wonderfully Made

A prayer of Mark Berryhill

She is undoubtedly one of God's greatest creations. She is pretty and she is on fire for the God whom she loves.

She prays and sings and is constantly acknowledging her love for her Creator.

She also is young and tender as her brother. She is a precious seven year old girl filled with a zest for life like her Father God.

She brings such joy into His life. The child is a creation of its own. He, the Almighty, is truly the giver of every good and perfect gift.

Dressed beautifully wearing a new soft blue and white dress she truly is an adorable creation.

Can you imagine what it must be like to know that the precious child is tucked safely into the heart of their Creator because of the sacrifice of the most precious Lamb ever created?

The Lamb of God bought you at His cross two thousand years ago. Love Him, serve Him and spend eternal paradise with Him my precious, precious baby girl.

As He is in the light so shall we walk. Walking in darkness brings God's wrath, destruction and damnation while walking in His light brings love, joy, peace, longsuffering, gentleness, goodness, faith, meekness and temperance.

The child truly is delicately and wonderfully created by a Father who loves them with all of His being.

In the name of the
Father, the Son and
the Holy Ghost

Amen and Amen
Copyright © 2008

128

The Gift of Life

A song of Mark Berryhill

Displayed across the Heavens is the most significant work of art that will ever be designed.

When the Creator of life painted with delicate but strong fingers the cross of His Son Jesus Christ, God the Father had a very special person in His mind.

The blood of the Lamb of God is our way back to our LORD. We were a lost and sinful people but the Father's called-out children walk in the light of His Son Jesus Christ.

To die in Christ Jesus will introduce us to the eternal victory that He won for you and I while He suffered pain and agony on the cross at Calvary.

He is the Alpha and He is the Omega. He is the Creator of love, life and laughter. He rejoices in His heart while His children cleave unto Him with all of their hearts.

The Holy Ghost is such a wonderful and powerful gift from God. The Holy Ghost is our friend. He will guide you in all truth. He will teach you how to walk the path God has set before you.

Love Him. Be attentive to His voice. He requires a willing vessel that walks with Him in true holiness and in true righteousness.

He is alive and He is on fire for Jesus. These children, these precious, precious children are His delight. As a good father constantly and consistently watches over and corrects his little ones so also is how He watches over the little lambs of God the Father.

Father, with You we are an invincible people. Father protect these little lambs against evil. Lead these precious baby lambs in the pathway of righteousness for Your great names sake.

Displayed across the Heavens is a picture painted by the most brilliant artist known to man. With delicate yet strong fingers He painted the masterpiece of all time.

YAHWEH is His name. The work of art painted by the unseen artist was painted because He had a very special and beloved person in mind.

He said, I love you, and I love you with all that I AM!

Love Me and serve Me with all that you are you very special and beloved child.

A tear of joy transforms into tears of joy running as a river, and a tear of thanksgiving likened unto a down pour of God's rain when one realizes the eternal victory Jesus Christ won for His children at His cross.

The unseen artist wept and cried, My Son, My Son, My Son where are You My Son?

All praise, glory, honor and power to the one who sits on the throne.

In the name of the
Father, the Son and
the Holy Ghost

Amen and Amen
Copyright © 2008

The Importance of Time

A prayer of Mark Berryhill

He is worthy to be praised because He is the Creator of life. He is worthy to be praised because He is the sustainer of life. He is worthy to be praised because He is the Savior of His people.

He carries the universe by His Word. There is power beyond human comprehension within the words that are so perfectly placed in His book known as the Holy Scriptures. The power and eternal victory is in the blood of God's precious Lamb Jesus Christ.

If we give of our time or money to others it is because we care about them and are created in the image and likeness of God. Time and how we invest the time that the Lord gives us is the most important factor of life.

How do you spend your time each day? Do you spend your time serving the Lord with diligent study, prayer and fasting?

He is a God and a Lord that is restricted neither by time or the amount of love He possesses.

Four hours of scripture memorization each day is to be considered the minimal. To read five Old Testament and five new Testament chapters each day is to be considered the minimal. Drink no less than seven glasses of water each day for health and memory retention.

God is Spirit and wants to be worshipped in Spirit and in truth. He wants to bless His people. He wants to give us good gifts.

For truly He is the giver of every good and perfect gift. His ear is attentive to the cries of His children. He is a Father who will never leave nor forsake His children.

For one to be prepared for the trials of life, one must be trained in The Word of God and in the Spirit. Eternal life in paradise with God is the true goal that is set before each one of us. Seek Him and love Him with all of your heart, your soul, your mind and your strength.

He answers the prayers of His saints. He is a Father who deserves all praise, glory, honor and power. He is the great I AM THAT I AM!

Men and women of faith become men and women of faith because they serve Him the way He desires to be served. He wants all of you. Your heart, your soul, your mind and strength are to be at His command.

There is true beauty in holiness. There is true beauty in righteousness. He is calling for a bridegroom that walks in the beauty of true holiness and righteousness.

You pray and He hears. You sing with love and joy in your heart for Him and it places love and joy in His heart.

Is the motive of the heart to be weighed? May the motive of our hearts be to train a world of children in the ways of the Almighty.

He is strength. He is power. He is the Eternal One

In the name of the
Father, the Son and
the Holy Ghost

Amen and Amen
Copyright © 2008

A Story of Faith

A song of Mark Berryhill

Is there anything that is too difficult for the Lord? Be still and consider carefully who He is. Is there anything that is too difficult for the Lord?

I see Him smile with a smile that reaches from the west even unto the east. I hear Him snicker at the thought of anything being too difficult for Him.

He is able to accomplish all things. Nothing ever has been or ever will be too difficult for Him.

The Father says to be fruitful and multiply.

Be holy as I AM holy.

Love your brothers and sisters as I love your brothers and sisters. Consider them as still being young and tender.

He clearly states, I AM love. My son, my precious son, write your Father's Word on the table of your heart each day that He provides you with the air that you breathe.

My daughter, my adorable daughter, write your Father's Word on the table of your heart each day that He provides you the breath of life.

Memorize His Holy Scriptures. Write His Word on the table of your hearts my precious son and my adorable daughter.

Enjoy life. Enjoy the beauty of His marvelous creation that so readily surrounds you. You truly are fearfully and wonderfully made creations. You my precious children are the delight and joy of His heart.

Faith in God is increased through the diligent study and memorization of His Holy Scriptures.

Why were you created? You were created to love and serve your Creator with all of your being.

His blessings are countless and untold for His called-out and obedient children. He truly is a rewarder to those who believe that He is and diligently seek Him.

Who are You Father? Who are You Lord Jesus? Who are You Holy Ghost? He responded clearly and precisely, I AM THAT I AM!

He will never tire of hearing you say that you love Him. He will never ever, ever, ever leave nor forsake you. He is faithful and is true.

As written aforetime, He is the way, the truth and the life. JESUS CHRIST is His name.

In the name of the
Father, the Son and
the Holy Ghost

Amen and Amen
Copyright © 2008

Thank Him for the Spirit of Thanksgiving

A prayer of Mark Berryhill

My Lord I will praise You with all that I am. O Lord I will love You with all of my being. My Lord, cause me to serve You with a pure and perfect heart.

Father, thank You for the Spirit of thanksgiving. Thank You for Your Son and for His accomplishment at the cross. Thank You for His blood that enables us to come boldly to Your throne of grace.

Father, thank You for Your holy angel that resides wherever Your predestinated children may be walking. Lord Jesus thank You for the Spirit of concentration and for the Spirit of memory retention.

Fill us with Your infinite love and Your marvelous and everlasting Word. By Your lead and by the gift of Your Spirit enable and cause Your chosen children to know Your Holy Scriptures better than any generation of Your children have ever known the everlasting Gospel.

Teach us and our children for days without end to love You with all of our hearts, souls, minds and strength. Make us to know the number of our days. Help us to remember that our days on the earth truly are but a vapor, a shadow and a mist.

Walk Your children in the power and love of Your Word and in the unlimited power of the Holy Ghost.

A petition offered to the Holy One of Israel by Your friend and servant.

In the name of the
Father, the Son and
the Holy Ghost

Amen and Amen
Copyright © 2008

The Bride and the Bridegroom

A prayer of Mark Berryhill

As the soothing comfort that is brought to the ear by the whisper of the wind as it glides through the pine trees which reach into Heaven, so is the comfort our God by His Holy Spirit brings forth to His children.

The running wind causes the trees to sing a song which brings forth peacefulness and beauty to the heart of this poor man.

By the hand of the Lord the poor man is quickly becoming a rich man. Poverty and wealth must be weighed by lack of faith and lack of works against mountains of faith and mountains of works which brings God treasures of love into His children's hearts.

His precious and free gift of grace is His treasure of love extended to His called-out children. He lives and dwells in the light and so as He lives and dwells in the light so will we walk in the light of Christ from this day and each day henceforth.

He is risen and He is coming. Prepare yourself and Your children as the holy bride which is to be accounted worthy to spend eternity with the bridegroom.

His mercy and His love is immeasurable. He is a Father, a Son and a Spirit that is victorious.

He sings songs of love and beauty while dancing with joy in His heart over you this very day because He loves you with all of His heart, with all of His soul, with all of His strength and with all of His mind.

Before I formed you in the womb of your mother, I anointed you as a king and a priest unto me. You are to be a holy man because I Am the Holy One of Israel.

I remember the beauty of the delivery as you departed from the body of the mother and entered into the world. I consider and remember the beauty of the birth of the precious child.

The true beauty is the child who was brought forth by He who is Faithful and He who is True.

His words are echoed throughout the world. Consider life. Consider death. Consider eternal life against eternal separation from the Creator of life.

It has been considered and it has been weighed and we will walk in holiness and righteousness until our death or until the return of the King of kings.

A drop of rain brings forth new hope. An abundance of God's rain brings forth blessings of the earth for whom it is prepared.

The Spirit of knowledge and understanding can only be found in His book which is called by one of His great names THE WORD OF GOD.

Can you describe the colors which are found in the rainbows of God?

In the name of the
Father, the Son and
the Holy Ghost

Amen and Amen

"His Precious Child"

By Mark Berryhill

Table of Contents

His Precious Child

A prayer of Mark Berryhill

Where were you when I spread forth the Heavens by the power of My right hand, My precious child?

Where were you when I set forth the boundaries of the great bodies of water, My precious child?

Where were you when I hung the moon and brilliant stars in the night sky, My precious child?

Where were you while My Beloved Son hung on the cross to pay for your sins and for the sins of the world, My precious child?

Where were you when I created the Heavens and the earth and the beauty they possess, tell me if you know, My precious child?

In the name of the
Father, the Son and
the Holy Ghost

Amen and Amen
Copyright © 2008

The Greatness of Jehovah

A prayer of Mark Berryhill

Jehovah, we thank You for sending an abundance of rain.

Jehovah, we thank You for the beauty You brought forth this day.

Jehovah, we thank You for our children, those we already have and those yet to be conceived.

Jehovah, cause Your greatness and light to be manifested throughout the Heavens and upon the earth.

Jehovah, we love You, we adore You, and we need You in all that we do.

In the name of the
Father, the Son and
the Holy Ghost

Amen and Amen
Copyright © 2008

His Infinite Wisdom

A prayer of Mark Berryhill

Life is good and the children of Christ never taste death.

Jehovah brings forth great joy into the hearts of His people when another precious child is born.

Immanuel is dancing in Heaven as the sound of the trumpet draws ever so near.

By our faith in Jesus we will overcome the world.

Secrets from God continue to be revealed to His servants, and yet many people rebel against His infinite wisdom.

In the name of the
Father, the Son and
the Holy Ghost

Amen and Amen
Copyright © 2008

By His Right Hand

A song of Mark Berryhill

The flowers cover the hill and appear as if they were designed by God to be a blanket for her.

The flowers are varied in color, and each flower is unique, even as the people God has placed on the earth.

Name the colors that you know, and a flourishing flower clothed in a beautiful dress can be found to match any color that comes to mind.

On the other side of the flowers, magnificent trees reach into heaven.

As the wind of God passes through the trees it is as though the trees in perfect unison, are glorifying their Creator in song.

In an open field in the midst of the trees a daddy, a mother, five little boys and twin girls are fishing for the first catch of the day.

In the name of the
Father, the Son and
the Holy Ghost

Amen and Amen
Copyright © 2008

Blessed is Our God

A song of Mark Berryhill

Blessed is the God of our Lord and Savior Jesus Christ.
Blessed is the Alpha and Omega.
Blessed is the Wonderful Counselor.
Blessed is the God of Abraham, father of a multitude.
Blessed is the Lion of Judah.
Blessed is the God over Israel.
Blessed is Jesus Christ, Light of the world.

In the name of the
Father, the Son and
the Holy Ghost

Amen and Amen
Copyright © 2008

The Brilliance of God

A song of Mark Berryhill

Mere words cannot describe the beauty God has bestowed upon the bride as she begins her approach to her soon to be husband.

Her elegance and beauty are manifested throughout the church and to all that are in attendance.

Her pure white dress is decorated with elegant beads, which appear to come to life as she gracefully positions herself next to the man God has ordained for her to marry.

The bridegroom, being awestruck by the beauty of his soon to be bride, gently holds her hands and begins the wedding vows.

As the vows are completed, the pastor, with love in his heart, gently tells the bridegroom that he may kiss his bride.

God is brilliant, He is good and in Him there is only the light Jesus Christ.

In the name of the
Father, the Son and
the Holy Ghost

Amen and Amen
Copyright © 2008

Simple Truth

A song of Mark Berryhill

Love causes the people of God to keep His commandments, while the lack thereof leads only to destruction.

Love soars on the wings of the angels of God, while hate buries the dead in their graves.

Love dances with faith, and children are the great rewards of God.

Love never fails, while hate never succeeds.

Love produces life, while hate seeks to destroy her.

Love produces precious children filled with the Spirit of God, and to love and serve God is the reason He created you.

In the name of the
Father, the Son and
the Holy Ghost

Amen and Amen
Copyright © 2008

By Design of the Father

A prayer of Mark Berryhill

Jesus came from heaven to earth and accomplished the work of the Father.

Jesus laid down His life for you because He loves you and because of His faith in His Father.

Jesus is the Light of the world and through His blood your eternal salvation rests securely with the Father.

Jesus is rejoicing in Heaven for your redemption is drawing near, says the Father.

In the name of the
Father, the Son and
the Holy Ghost

Amen and Amen
Copyright © 2008

Pure Love

A song of Mark Berryhill

A lazy man will not work in cold weather, and yet the same man will soon be pleading for food and shelter.

Obedience is more valued to God than sacrifice, while the lack of obedience eventually steals the very joy of living.

It has been written that money answers all things, and yet truly it is only pure love that can be accredited with answering all things.

If you fear death, you lack understanding; the children of God are washed in the redeeming blood of Jesus Christ.

If there is sin in your life, denounce the sin and turn from her, God has no pleasure in wickedness.

In the name of the
Father, the Son and
the Holy Ghost

Amen and Amen
Copyright © 2008

King of Victory

A prayer of Mark Berryhill

Dedication to perfect practice produces excellence, while lack thereof produces defeat.

Do you run a race to win the prize, or do you run the race to lose?

Victory is not only deserved by the first place runner, she also belongs to each person who gave everything that they had during the race.

For others, the mere attempting of the race alone represents victory.

There was a man sent from Heaven to earth by God, His name translated is King of Victory!

In the name of the
Father, the Son and
the Holy Ghost

Amen and Amen
Copyright © 2008

Jesus Christ is Lord

A song of Mark Berryhill

The practice of righteousness brings forth righteousness, while ungodliness is brought forth by those who practice ungodliness.

The diligent study of the Word of God teaches the simple wisdom and understanding, while the lack thereof brings forth destruction.

A nation whose children seek God daily through the diligent study of His Word will be exalted, while the nation who ignores the Word of God will be utterly destroyed.

Life is as a calm cool night with brilliant shining stars; she is to be enjoyed to the fullest, walking in the light of Jesus Christ.

In the name of the
Father, the Son and
the Holy Ghost

Amen and Amen
Copyright © 2008

God with Us

A song of Mark Berryhill

The precious child born to the beautiful virgin would eventually be called to carry the government upon His shoulders.

The precious child born to the beautiful virgin is the Son of God.

The birth of the precious child that was born in a manger was the most important birth that will ever be known to the human race.

The precious child, born to the beautiful virgin, was the only one found worthy by the Father, and through His blood, and His blood alone, salvation is found.

The precious child grew up and became known as Immanuel, which being interpreted is God with us.

In the name of the
Father, the Son and
the Holy Ghost

Amen and Amen
Copyright © 2008

Jehovah is Love

A song of Mark Berryhill

Love keeps no record of wrongs, and mercy rests in the right hand of God.

Hate seeks to destroy life, while love procreates her.

Joy is brought forth into the hearts of both the mother and the father at the birth of their new child.

Misery is shed forth because of disobedience to the Word of God.

Peace is greater and preferred above war, although there is a time and place for both war and peace.

Love is faithful when all else fails, and your Creator, He is love!

In the name of the
Father, the Son and
the Holy Ghost

Amen and Amen
Copyright © 2008

All about Him

A song of Mark Berryhill

A nation that seeks God and His righteousness daily will be exalted, while the nation failing to do so will soon cease to exist.

True wealth of individuals is found in the amount of love they possess for Jesus Christ and others, not in their earthly possessions.

A wife possessing a beautiful heart and precious children are gifts from God.

It is a great day indeed when good people accept Jesus Christ as their personal Savior, and commit their lives to serving Him.

In the name of the
Father, the Son and
the Holy Ghost

Amen and Amen
Copyright © 2008

Life Eternal

A song of Mark Berryhill

Never underestimate the amount of love Jehovah has placed within His heart for you.

When all else may have failed, remember that it is the angel of Jehovah that will strengthen you.

Jehovah spoke and created light, can you?

Children are the great rewards of Jehovah and the delight of His heart.

Jehovah is from everlasting to everlasting and within His right hand your eternal salvation securely rests.

In the name of the
Father, the Son and
the Holy Ghost

Amen and Amen
Copyright © 2008

Success over Failure

A song of Mark Berryhill

Obedience to the Word of God causes abundance, while the lack thereof promotes destruction.

Placing faith in Jesus Christ for your eternal salvation is the most important decision of ones life.

Love conquers, subdues and rules over evil; therefore one is to never be without hope.

Life is a gift from God and His angels have been commanded to care for His children.

Good health is likewise a blessing from God, remember to treat your body for what it is, the tabernacle of God.

In the name of the
Father, the Son and
the Holy Ghost

Amen and Amen
Copyright © 2008

Whisper of Jehovah

A prayer of Mark Berryhill

Jehovah whispers and the dry desolate land becomes as a brilliant painting with everything covered by snow.

Jesus is dancing in Heaven as our time to be with Him in Heaven is drawing ever so near.

Jehovah is singing songs of beauty in Heaven about us because He is faithful and His love will endure throughout infinity.

Jesus won the victory for you and I at the cross, His precious blood paid the price for our eternal salvation.

In the name of the
Father, the Son and
the Holy Ghost

Amen and Amen
Copyright © 2008

Women of Faith

A song of Mark Berryhill

A godly wife is a blessing from God, while an ungodly wife is as a thorn constantly stabbing your side.

A godly wife conceives and procreates children of faith while an ungodly woman considers only herself.

A godly woman, that fears God, is to be admired, while an ungodly woman has no respect for her husband.

A woman of faith is a gift to her husband, while a woman lacking faith is as a poisonous viper prepared to strike.

In the name of the
Father, the Son and
the Holy Ghost

Amen and Amen
Copyright © 2008

Exalt the Lord

A prayer of Mark Berryhill

The view of the majestic waterfall is overwhelming and causes us once again to appreciate the brilliance with which God created the Heavens and the earth.

The waterfall is singing songs of beauty while dancing with the precision of a ballerina as she performs her greatest performance.

The cold winter will soon be gone and beautiful flowers will once again be clothed in delicate dresses of velvet.

The sun, moon and stars are attentive to the voice of their Creator, and follow His plan; why are your ears closed to His voice and heart hardened at His command?

In the name of the
Father, the Son and
the Holy Ghost

Amen and Amen
Copyright © 2008

Light Versus Darkness

A song of Mark Berryhill

The hometown basketball team has a commanding lead at halftime, and special halftime activities are about to begin.

The baton babes are young girls ranging from about three years of age up to seventeen.

The girls are dressed cute and are a blessing to watch as they skillfully twirl their batons as if the batons have been with them all their lives.

The dance teams of two local schools now begin to perform. They, on the other hand, are dressed improperly and their suggestive dancing brings great disappointment into my heart.

The hometown team continues to lead the game up until about the last minute, but then suddenly find themselves where their opponent had been all night long, losing on the scoreboard.

With three seconds left, a player for the hometown team shoots what may be a game winning basket, unfortunately the ball rolls off the rim rather than into the rim.

In the name of the
Father, the Son and
the Holy Ghost

Amen and Amen
Copyright © 2008

Within the Heart of a Man

A song of Mark Berryhill

The birds are singing because the sun is shining brightly and the long cold winter is drawing to a close.

Some trees are being clothed in new dresses, while others will be wearing new suits.

The sound of joy and laughter from children playing blesses the neighborhoods.

Divine protection is ordered when children are fed the Word of God daily in the public schools and not withheld when they are not.

Unwise and foolish men are soon removed from positions of authority.

In the name of the
Father, the Son and
the Holy Ghost

Amen and Amen
Copyright © 2008

Peace and Joy

A song of Mark Berryhill

The dry barren land is once again refreshed with an abundance of rain because of the faithfulness of God.

The perfect rain will cause the trees to dance and the flowers to sing new songs.

The grass and shrubs glisten with a new sparkle and even the air is fresher on this beautiful day of the Lord.

The magnificent rainbow brings peace and joy into the heart of this man.

In the name of the
Father, the Son and
the Holy Ghost

Amen and Amen
Copyright © 2008

Everlasting Father

A song of Mark Berryhill

Tears of joy from the eyes of Jehovah have filled the oceans because of His immense love for His people Israel.

Jehovah reigns over Heaven and earth, and beside Him there is no other.

Jehovah, You are our strength and our song, bless Your lambs.

Immanuel is the Beginning and the End, for He is the Everlasting Father.

In the name of the
Father, the Son and
the Holy Ghost

Amen and Amen
Copyright © 2008

Alpha and Omega

A prayer of Mark Berryhill

A nation that uses time properly will be victorious, while rebellious nations ultimately self-destruct.

Children are gifts from God and they are the delight of His heart; consider that their angels do always behold the face of the Almighty.

A godly wife is likewise a present from God; cherish her as Christ loves His people.

Wealth is good if used properly and evil when used improperly.

Jesus Christ is the Beginning and the End.

In the name of the
Father, the Son and
the Holy Ghost

Amen and Amen
Copyright © 2008

I AM

A prayer of Mark Berryhill

Will you ever learn to trust I AM my precious child?

Will you ever understand that I AM will never leave nor forsake you my precious child.

I AM knew the time of your conception before He laid the foundations of the earth.

I AM is from everlasting to everlasting, and I AM is your strength and strong tower.

I AM THAT I AM delivered His children in the days of Pharaoh, king of Egypt, and He will deliver you today!

In the name of the
Father, the Son and
the Holy Ghost

Amen and Amen
Copyright © 2008

By Faith in Jesus

A prayer of Mark Berryhill

Rejoice and be glad for His tomb is empty!

Rejoice and be glad for He paid the price of your sins!

Rejoice and be glad for His love and faithfulness is from everlasting to everlasting!

Rejoice and be glad for your God is love!

Rejoice and be glad for as the Father raised the Son, so will the Son raise you!

In the name of the
Father, the Son and
the Holy Ghost

Amen and Amen
Copyright © 2008

A Victorious Father

A prayer of Mark Berryhill

A godly wife is a gift from God, and children are His great reward.

Spiritual insight is worth more than gold or silver and yet love is the greatest of all.

Place your faith in God and He will use you to conquer the world in His name.

As the Father raised the Son from the tomb, so likewise will the Son raise those who have placed their faith in Him.

Tears of joy from the eyes of JEHOVAH have filled His oceans and the American Bald Eagle soars on the wings of His angels.

In the name of the
Father, the Son and
the Holy Ghost

Amen and Amen
Copyright © 2008

Creator, Savior, Sustainer

A prayer of Mark Berryhill

Jehovah makes the sun to rise and then causes her to rest.

Jehovah hung the earth in mid air and painted the boundaries of her great bodies of water.

Jehovah loves you with all of His heart, soul, mind and strength; do you love Him in the same manner?

Jehovah is great, and besides Him there is no other.

Jehovah listens to the birds sing and knows every thought of your heart!

In the name of the
Father, the Son and
the Holy Ghost

Amen and Amen
Copyright © 2008

Beloved Child of the Lord

A song of Mark Berryhill

Beloved Child of the Lord, in your fast you will discover great comfort, and your Father will be faithful to send an abundance of His rain.

Beloved child of the Lord, in life you may find obstacles and difficulty, but be of good cheer, your Savior has overcome the world!

Beloved child of the Lord, seek God with all of your heart and He will be readily found!

Beloved child of the Lord, submit your spirit to the lead of the Holy Spirit and watch Jehovah subdue the nations of the world under His feet!

Hallelujah, Hallelujah, Hallelujah!

In the name of the
Father, the Son and
the Holy Ghost

Amen and Amen
Copyright © 2008

Blessed of God

A prayer of Mark Berryhill

A godly wife is a gift from God; love her as He loves His church.

Children are the great rewards of God, and their angels do always behold the face of the Almighty.

Gentleness is greater than strength, for with gentleness the children of Israel are led by God.

Victory is preferred over defeat and self-discipline promotes victory.

The just live by faith, while the unjust have yet to find her.

In the name of the
Father, the Son and
the Holy Ghost

Amen and Amen
Copyright © 2008

God Bless the World

A song of Mark Berryhill

Water is resting in the low area of beautiful pastures because God has been faithful once again to pour down His rain.

The cattle are satisfied because of the large quantity of grass to eat and the horses likewise are content.

Magnificent fields have been prepared by the hard work of farmers and prosperity appears to be within the clutch of a hand.

Why are mothers not appreciated every day as on this day?

Entering into the large city, one cannot help but notice the brilliant sign placed at the entrance of the city; God bless the world!

In the name of the
Father, the Son and
the Holy Ghost

Amen and Amen
Copyright © 2008

The Defeated Grave

A prayer of Mark Berryhill

Father, we will seek Your face from the rising of the sun until the closing of our eyelids.

Even in the night watch, with eyelids closed, we will seek You as You reveal marvelous dreams to us during our sleep.

Father, do You ever need to rest from all of Your majestic works?

Father, thank You for life and love, but most of all thank You for painting the resurrection of Your Son Jesus Christ from the grave that was unable to hold Him!

In the name of the
Father, the Son and
the Holy Ghost

Amen and Amen
Copyright © 2008

Child of God

A prayer of Mark Berryhill

Jehovah brought forth the gift of life for the human race out of the dust of the earth, and by breathing life into Adam.

Jesus offers each one of us the gift of eternal life; accept Him for who He is, the Son of the true and living God.

Holy Spirit, shine forth brilliantly in the children of God, today and for all of the tomorrows.

Jehovah reigns over Heaven and earth, and besides Him there is no other!

Jesus is love and His heart leaps for joy at the birth of His children!

Holy Spirit, shine forth brilliantly in the children of God, today and for all of the tomorrows.

In the name of the
Father, the Son and
the Holy Ghost

Amen and Amen
Copyright © 2008

Your Word

A prayer of Mark Berryhill

Be faithful to direct the steps of Your children Almighty Father, for we have acknowledged You!

Remember the covenant You established with Abraham, Isaac and Jacob, Your greatly beloved.

JEHOVAH, be faithful to remember mercy during wrath, and kindness during anger.

Father, be slow to anger; extend Your loving hand to a gainsaying people and forgive.

Lord Jesus, let Your light shine in the hearts of Your children, and may their every thought be brought into the captivity of Your Word.

In the name of the
Father, the Son and
the Holy Ghost

Amen and Amen
Copyright © 2008

Glorify Jesus

A prayer of Mark Berryhill

The sun presents his beauty and warmth once again, and the moon gives her light in the cool of nights.

Precious and beautiful children are majestically clothed this morning, for they know it is the day of their God.

Loving parents one day will come to the realization that every day is the day of their children's God.

If you want the blessings of God, learn what He requires of you and obey Him.

In the name of the
Father, the Son and
the Holy Ghost

Amen and Amen
Copyright © 2008

From the Heart

A song of Mark Berryhill

Father, thank You for providing another beautiful day, whereby we can serve You.

Father, thank You for the gift of eternal life.

Lord Jesus, thank You for the victory You won for Your people at the cross of Calvary.

Father God, thank You for raising Jesus from the grave.

Father, thank You for faithful mothers and fathers.

Father, thank You!

In the name of the
Father, the Son and
the Holy Ghost

Amen and Amen
Copyright © 2008

Pure and Perfect Heart

A prayer of Mark Berryhill

Jesus Christ was with the Father before the creation of the world, for He is the Great I AM!

If you are hurting and seem to have no where to turn, place your eyes upon Jesus, He is faithful and true.

If you desire a life filled with joy and goodness, serve Jesus with a pure and perfect heart.

In the name of the
Father, the Son and
the Holy Ghost

Amen and Amen
Copyright © 2008

The Good Shepherd

A prayer of Mark Berryhill

Jesus Christ is alive and He rules and reigns over the hearts of His children.

Jesus Christ offers eternal paradise by simply believing in Him and obeying Him.

Jesus Christ is faithful and true; He will never leave or forsake you.

Jesus Christ is unchanging; by His blood your eternal salvation is secure.

Jesus Christ is the Good Shepherd, and besides Him there is no other!

In the name of the
Father, the Son and
the Holy Ghost

Amen and Amen
Copyright © 2008

Faithful and True

A song of Mark Berryhill

Where is the dwelling place of the God of Israel?

Where is the God that led the children of Israel out of the bondage of the Egyptians?

If you know wise friend, tell me where the God of Israel resides?

Is not your heart the dwelling place of the God of Israel, my beloved child?

Is not your heart the dwelling place of the Most High, my beloved child?

He is with you, and He will never leave you nor forsake you; He is faithful and He is true.

In the name of the
Father, the Son and
the Holy Ghost

Amen and Amen
Copyright © 2008

Serve Christ Today

A prayer of Mark Berryhill

Did you extend love, help and hope to your neighbors in their time of need, or did you look the other way and pretend not to see?

Have you truly given your heart to Jesus Christ, and submitted to His lead, or are you still walking in the spirit of the rebellion?

Are the children prepared for the sound of the trumpet of God, or are they seeking the ungodly things of this world?

Listen, the end is ever so near; teach the lambs of Christ His Word while there is a today.

In the name of the
Father, the Son and
the Holy Ghost

Amen and Amen
Copyright © 2008

The Common Bond

Table of Contents

He Died for you, and He Died for Me

A prayer of Mark Berryhill

Always consider the other person better than yourself, his Savior died for him.

Never underestimate the power of God. He is love and He is wrath!

"There is no fear in love; but perfect love casts out fear, because fear has torment. He that fears is not made perfect in love."[16]

Praise the other person and not yourself, her Savior died for her.

Love is our desire.

In God there is hope for the hurting. In Him there is hope of eternal life.

In Him, and with Him, I can do all things. In Him, and with Him, you can do all things.

I am weak and He is strong. He is holy.

His great Word has the power to heal the nation that is lost.

With His Spirit, and by His Word, He can do all things.

My precious son, and my daughter, write the Word of God upon the table of your hearts.

How can a person show how much love He has for another person? How is it possible for anyone to show you how much He loves you by allowing Himself to be hung on a tree for you?

With blood dripping from thorns placed within His innocent head, He died for you and He died for me.

In the name of the
Father, the Son and
the Holy Ghost

Amen and Amen
Copyright © 2008

---

[16] King James Version I John 4:8

God is Faithful

A prayer of Mark Berryhill

Consider who God is.

God rules over the universe with the Word of God and with His Holy Spirit.

God is our love, our life and our light.

God is our daily and eternal provision.

He is enduring and uncompromising faithfulness.

Nothing or no one can snatch the children of God out of His hand.

He walks with me and He talks with me. Whether I am happy or sad, He is with me.

God is faithful.

May my son and my daughter dwell in the beauty of the holiness of the Lord God Almighty forevermore.

In the name of the
Father, the Son and
the Holy Ghost

Amen and Amen
Copyright © 2008

To Covet the Gift of Prophecy

A prayer of Mark Berryhill

It is a joy living for the King. The joy of serving faithfully the King of kings, the Lord of Lords is wonderful.

Goodness, love and truth are but a few words that describe our Lord.

Jesus, teach us the way You want us to be. Write Your Word in our minds and in our hearts.

Wait, listen and consider who God is.

He is life. He is in Heaven and He is in hell.

There is no life without God in our lives. He is our all in all.

God is the giver of the breath of life, and God is the extinguisher of the breath of life.

We are flesh. We are Spirit. We are God's, provided we walk according to His Word.

Meditate on His Word day and night. Pray continually without ceasing.

Keep yourself pure and holy. Walk blamelessly before the God of all things.

Teach me to war for You with words You allow my fingers to write.

Courage, be strong and of good courage. He has promised to never leave nor forsake His children.

The sting of death! Where was the sting of death?

Transform us into the likeness of the King. Wash our minds with the pure water of Your Word.

Covet the gift of prophecy. Covet purity. Covet God.

Lord Jesus, help us to be perfect in both the flesh and Spirit. Help us to love You with all of our being.

Write Your Word on the hearts and minds of these precious

people. The people of God are a peculiar people. We are His possession.

Self discipline, self-restraint and work are blessings from God.
Come and heal Your people Israel my Lord and my King.
Mold us, hold us, disciple us and love us.

In the name of the
Father, the Son and
the Holy Ghost

Amen and Amen
Copyright © 2008

The Beauty of Little Boys and Little Girls

A prayer of Mark Berryhill

Violet, soft yellow. Yellow. Dainty Yellow.

Ceniza, pretty. Soft green.

Thank You for the beautiful selection of colors You gave us Lord Jesus.

As the joy the virgin bride knows as she walks the walkway to marriage, and as the excitement and love the young virgin boy feels as He walks the pathway to marriage, so is the joy, excitement, and love our Lord has for each of His children.

Purity, holiness, godliness and righteousness walk hand in hand.

When God says that He will never leave you nor forsake you, He stands by His words.

How much love can one mother have for her daughter? How much love can one man have for his son?

We are for but one reason. We are to love. Give us love my Lord and my God.

Father, I love You!

Jesus, I love You!

Holy Spirit, I love You!

Knowledge, understanding and wisdom are but a few of our Lord's traits.

Why is the earth called earth and the sea called sea?

Honesty, judgment, justice and mercy. Grace and love beyond mans mental capacity.

It is a mystery to fathom that God carries all of these people with His mighty hand.

Remember to meditate on God's Word day and night without ceasing.

Dresses of beauty for little girls. Love and laughter. Friendship of the innocent.

Dresses of beauty for little girls. Young and tender. Babies, children. Young and beautiful girls in dresses with all of the colors in the world.

Young boys, future men. Young and so tender. Brilliant and so often taken for granted.

Nurture and love your precious son. Love and nurture your precious daughter.

Son and daughter of the Most High, write His Word in your hearts and minds.

Inquisitive, assertive and a bit lackadaisical but handsome.

Inquisitive, assertive and not a bit lackadaisical but beautiful.

Love, nurture, teach and listen to your child. Gently mold him into a child of God. Gently mold her into a child of God.

My Father, You are such a joy to this poor man. My Lord Jesus my friend, You are such a joy to this rich man.

Visible and invisible, the world is governed by the King of Israel.

Birthday parties for little girls. Birthday parties for little boys. Blessings untold and too often take for granted.

Thank You for these precious children You have loaned us for this short time our Lord, our God and our King.

Hearts of gold, hearts of silver. Hearts of love. Hearts of faithfulness and suddenly we see we are created in the image and likeness of Your Father God Almighty and my Father God Almighty.

In the name of the
Father, the Son and
the Holy Ghost

Amen and Amen
Copyright © 2008

Life Everlasting

A song of Mark Berryhill

The Word of God causes victory over the war that is fought in the secret places of the mind in the struggle between flesh and Spirit. Pray and fast.

As Jesus spoke the Spirit is willing but the flesh is weak, but then I remember that I have crucified the lust of the flesh for I am a child of the King.

Undying love. Faithful and true. Jesus Christ is His name. We who are Christ's have learned to walk in the Spirit. Perfect, perfect and without defilement.

Enjoy life and walk in the pathway of godliness.

Love and forgive and inherit a blessing from God.

There is but one reason for life. The reason for life is to learn God's Word and to obey God's Word.

In the name of the
Father, the Son and
the Holy Ghost

Amen and Amen
Copyright © 2008

The God who can do all Things

A prayer of Mark Berryhill

Father, thank You for today. Thank You for Your Son Jesus. Jesus, how are You this day?

God of joy, God of love and life and laughter! In happiness I will spend eternity!

Jesus, how are You today? I love You! Father, how are You today? Teach us Your Word and be involved in our daily lives.

Father, I know that You can do all things. Father, as Your child and as one of Your sons I ask You to teach these precious children Your Word from childhood until death.

Bless us with the wisdom and knowledge to diligently study Your Word every day.

In health and in sickness I will praise my God. In love and in laughter, and in joy I will praise my King.

In trouble and in difficulty I will extol the Holy One of God.

Lord God help us not to get too busy for You. Help us to spend our lives serving You! In order for this to happen You have to help.

Father, I sure enjoy provoking You and Jesus unto love and good works!

Jesus, our Daddy sure is strict. I love Him anyway! Besides He can kill this body and put this soul in eternal hell! Therefore I will walk uprightly!

Father, You and Jesus are neat. You both bring us a lot of joy. Your Word is great Lord God.

Father, thank You!

In the name of the
Father, the Son and
the Holy Ghost

Amen and Amen
Copyright © 2008

The Eternal One

A prayer of Mark Berryhill

Father, we want for You to be our Father, our Lord and our God.

Father, give me a giving heart and a caring heart. Give me a loving and beautiful heart.

My friend seemed slow and yet I was the one who was slow. My friend walked with a purpose! He had work to complete.

My friend gave His life so we can spend eternity with Him.

Moses and Elijah told Jesus that this is what He had come to accomplish.

We are temporal and we are eternal. Within our hearts and minds God will write His Word.

There is a world to evangelize for the King of kings. I pray that You will raise up laborers for Your harvest, Lord of the harvest.

In the name of the
Father, the Son and
the Holy Ghost

Amen and Amen
Copyright © 2008

In God's Strength the Children Rest

A prayer of Mark Berryhill

Rising early my daughter noticed the beauty of God's new day. "Daddy", she said, as she looked at the sun as it was slowly rising, "God sure can paint beautifully."

It is a gift from God to be able to see the beauty in all things. The secret is to love even though you may not be loved, and to care for the other person when no one else will.

Father, may we learn to see beauty in all things, and to see Your face at all times and in all things.

Father, it is wonderful to be able to teach about Your Son to the world. What a delight it is to be able to write a story about the King of kings.

You are loved by the Creator of the universe. He has commanded His holy angel to protect you. It is truly a special gift from God to be able to teach the teachings of our Lord and Savior Jesus Christ.

Father, teach us who You truly are and what You stand for. He responds, I will stand for You because I have already died for you.

As He has died for you and I, be prepared to die for Him.

We are bought and purchased with the blood of the King.

Glorify God in your Spirit and in your flesh. Walk with Jesus. Walk for Jesus. Turn the erring world to the King of kings.

In love there is responsibility, and in love there is keeping of commandments. In love and in life we will pursue the Most High.

Our children bring such gentleness and love to God. In His heart, in His mind, in His soul, and in His strength they rest.

The children are His great reward.

"Jehovah," the young boy calls out! "Jehovah," the young boy calls out!

"Abraham, Abraham," as the child rings out! Friend of the Most High.

Consider eternal life. Consider the temporal verses the eternal. Dwell in God's Word. Meditate and live and feed on the Word of the Most High.

Feed the lambs of Christ with His good Word. Gently and caringly write God's Word on the table of their hearts.

A wave, "Daddy, daddy," as the child sings out! A wave and a sign of love.

Kind, gentle, caring, trustworthy, honest and beautiful. So are the ways of God's children.

Walk in the light. Walk in obedience to the King of kings.

He is love! He is wrath!

Father, thank You for Jesus. Father, thank You for these precious children. Father, Son and Holy Ghost please write Your Word on the table of the hearts and minds of these beautiful, loving and great children.

In the name of the
Father, the Son and
the Holy Ghost

Amen and Amen
Copyright © 2008

Hearts of Love, Hearts of Gold, Hearts of Silver

A prayer of Mark Berryhill

Hearts of love. Hearts of gold. Hearts of silver. Our hearts are to be trained as Christ's heart was trained.

Retain the Word in your heart. Seek the face of our King. Glorify Jesus with perfection in both body and Spirit. Crucify lusts of the flesh.

We who belong to the King walk in the Spirit and not in the flesh.

Love, kindness, gentleness, life and light, the beauty of God's child.

Work, but stay in the Word; better yet let us make the Word our work.

Jesus, we love You! Jesus we need You in our daily lives. Jesus we adore You!

You are ours and we are yours. Father, we thank You for life and thank You for eternal victory.

Spirit, teach us to deny ourselves. Teach us to pick up our cross daily and follow where Jesus will lead us.

A son and a daughter, how can we be so blessed? How can we be so loved?

What a joy it is to receive Jesus as our Savior, and the gift of our beautiful children.

God is wonderful. He is great. He is love. He is light. He is life.

Gentle and so kind. Teach the child while he is alert and ready to learn. Father, please teach these precious children Your Word each day.

Help them to not only study Your great Word each day, but to also retain Your great Word on the table of their hearts.

Father, how much do you love Your children? Father, love us with all of Your heart, with all of Your soul, with all of Your mind and with all of Your strength.

With love there is risk. With love you can be hurt. With love you can move mountains. With love and in love with Jesus, you can reign and govern eternally.

Self control of mind and self control of flesh. Self control of all things.

O Lord God, thank You for the time we spend together. O Lord God, thank You for Emmanuel.

O Lord our Lord, there is a world that desires for You to be their God, their Father and their King.

The eyes of God roam the earth continually. He is omnipotent.

To retain one must learn. For one to learn and retain, time must be properly allocated.

Lord Jesus, Lord God, Holy Spirit, give us wisdom in the management of our time.

Father, we pray for the Spirit of love and for the Spirit of wisdom to do good at all times and in all things.

Trees. Planets. The beautiful fragrance of God's roses. Remember why we are here. We are here to serve the Most High.

Father, I love You! Jesus, I love You! Spirit, I love You!

Father, we love You! Jesus we love You! Spirit we love You!

Love us. Teach us Your Word every day my Lord and my God.

Jesus protect these children and place them under the shadow of Your wing.

To understand love. To understand wisdom. To know love. To know wisdom, to fear God and keep His commandments.

Weigh the temporal against the eternal. To abide in the light. To resist the temporal pleasures of this world for the eternal reward of Heaven.

Weigh eternity. Weigh the temporal. A man hopes for what he has not seen. A woman hopes for what she has not seen.

The child is the great reward of our God! He holds them and shapes them with His loving hands. O the love and wisdom God will reveal to mankind.

In life there are obstacles and trials; and yet without trials how would we know to appreciate the good?

May we see holiness and God in all things and at all times.

Look and admire the smile of the child. Look at the innocence of Gods child. It is a joy to know that he is loved by God. It is a joy to know that she is loved by God.

Know that God is their Father. Know that He has prepared their eternal home for them.

Father, thank You for the gift of life! Father, thank You for Jesus! Father, thank You for eternal life!

How great is Your love for these precious children my Lord and my God? Unmeasureable is my God's love for His children.

Purity, holiness, godliness and righteousness; these are the traits we pursue. God You are great and You are wonderful! I know because I love God, we know this because we love God.

We are the children of the Most High God.

Each day man perishes without regarding, and yet the Spirit of God's faithful children is renewed day by day.

We are flesh and we are Spirit. The Spirit lives eternally. Let us walk in obedience to Christ. Let us walk in the light.

The sword of the Spirit. The Word of God.

There is no knowledge or wisdom but the knowledge and wisdom God shares with His children.

God is love. God is light. God is life. In Him there is no darkness. In Him there is only light.

Lord Jesus, thank You for the gift of the Holy Spirit.

Father, thank You for Your Son. Father, cradle these beautiful and precious children in your bosom.

They belong to You. Love them. Mold them. Teach them Your Word my Lord and my God. Love. Beauty. White, soft yellow, red, burgundy and pink. Colors of beauty.

Father, the children are Your great reward. Mold them with Your skillful hands and with Your Holy Spirit my Lord and my God.

Peace. Honor. Truth. Uprightness of heart. Purity of flesh and Spirit.

Eyes of love. Eyes of innocence. Eyes that care. Eyes that share.

Charity above all things reigns with Jesus.

He is love. He is life. He provides the light.

O Lord our LORD, how great and marvelous You are!

Time is short. Time is eternity. Walk hand in hand with Your Lord. He is Spirit. He is eternal life.

Teach us to walk in the Spirit all of the days of our lives, our Lord and our God.

Patience, readiness of mind and evangelism.

JEHOVAH, Jesus and Holy Spirit, one and the same. Mystery of death, and yet there is no mystery to either life or death.

From conception to death, God is unchanging. For His children He will move mountains. For His children He gave Himself.

How can a person fight against love? How can a person pursue anything but Jesus?

We will pursue the Lord all of the days of our life. We will pursue and obey our Lord.

For His children, there are blessings untold. For His children, He will command His angels. For His children, He gave His life.

Struggles are part of life. Jesus Christ is a faithful High Priest.

Walk in the Spirit and not in the flesh. Walk for Christ, rather run for Christ.

Jesus, we love You! Jesus, we need You! Jesus, we adore You!

He reigns over the universe. His name is Jesus, King of kings and Lord of lords.

Love simplicity. There is no defense against love. Love conquers all things. Love is the reason God spares our lives each day. Love is the reason God takes many home each day. He never tires. He rises early and instructs His own in the way of righteousness.

He is my Father and I am one of His many children.

A kind word. A simple hello. A beautiful smile.

As Solomon wrote in Ecclesiastes 12:13, "Let us hear the conclusion of the whole matter: fear God and keep His commandments: for this is the whole duty of man."[17]

Compassion, tender mercies, faithfulness and unfailing love. Lord of lords is His name.

Father, how are You this day? Lord Jesus, how are You this day? Holy Spirit, how are You this day?

He responds by saying, joyful and excited about today and tomorrow! How could you not be when there are so many beautiful children born today and tomorrow?

---

[17] King James Version Ecclesiastes 12:13

O the infinite love and wisdom of my Father God. In Him we live and move and have our existence.

To the only wise God. Immortal, eternal and invisible. King of kings and Lord of lords.

A kind word. A gentle hello. A beautiful smile. Hearts of love. Hearts of gold. Hearts of silver. Hearts created in the image and likeness of the Creator.

Our bodies are the tabernacle of JEHOVAH God. Our bodies are the temple of the living God.

Walk in the Spirit and not in the flesh.

Precious are God's children in His eyes. How could we not be? He created and made us as He is.

Anger rests in the bosoms of fools. Love, forgiveness and compassion rest in the heart of the Creator.

Follow after obedience.

In the name of the
Father, the Son and
the Holy Ghost

Amen and Amen
Copyright © 2008

Learn His Word, Live His Word, Teach His Word

A prayer of Mark Berryhill

God softens my heart and then He makes it as cold and as hard as ice.

He has such fun with His children; I know He is joyful. I know He is love. I know He is mine and I know that you are His.

A faithful Father. A faithful Son. A faithful friend.

We fret about so many unnecessary things, when all we have to do is to let God fret over everything.

Laughter has been said to cure the soul, it is a blessing from the Father of lights too often taken for granted.

Father, thank You for listening to our prayers. Thank You for being alert and attentive to Your child.

There is a time to laugh and there is a time to cry. There is a time to love and there is a time to forgive.

Confess your sins and God will heal you faster than you can imagine.

God is Spirit. He knows all things. He created all things.

Concerning an important issue. Concerning eternal life, make no mistake, each one of us will give an account to Christ for our actions.

To do what is right, what is just, what is fair; one must have God's Word written in His heart.

Time is precious. Time is short. Use the time the Almighty gives You wisely.

Learn His Word. Live His Word. Teach His Word.

Jesus gave a commandment: "Go and teach all nations baptizing them in the name of the Father, and of the Son and of the Holy Ghost: Teaching them to observe all things, whatsoever I commanded you;

and lo, I am with you always, even until the end of the world. Amen"[18]

Let us realize the Lord Jesus Christ's goal. Let us go into every nation baptizing them in the name of the Father, and of the Son and of the Holy Ghost, and teach ourselves and others to observe all things Jesus has commanded, and lo, He will be with us, even until the end of the world. Amen.

When I consider how wonderful and powerful God is, it truly amazes me.

To know that I am His. To know that my children are His. To know that we must walk in the light. To know that there is a reward for obedience to Christ, and an eternal penalty for disobedience.

To give ones heart to the Lord is a wonderful decision. The home He has prepared for those who love Him and obey His commandments is worth running the race to win the prize.

Be creative. Be a teacher. Be as Jesus. Teach in parables. What a mystery it is to know that He will carry You and Your loved ones if and when they need to be carried.

The elder said that we must change our thought process. How true and how accurate are the words that He spoke.

We must learn to love each other the way the Lord loves His children.

Faithful and true. Jesus Christ is His name. Love Him and serve Him in the good times and in the bad times, for it is more blessed to give than to receive.

In the name of the
Father, the Son and
the Holy Spirit

Amen and Amen
Copyright © 2008

---

[18] King James Version Matthew 28:18-20

God is our Faithful Father

A prayer of Mark Berryhill

Life passes so quickly. Yesterday we were held in our mother's arms. Today we hold our children in our arms. And yet in all reality, my Father God is who has placed these children in His bosom. His love exceeds light. His greatness exceeds all things.

There is no defense against ones love for their child. God has blessings beyond human comprehension for His children. The river of God is always full. I suppose the fullness of the river is God's love for His child.

With God, with Jesus, with the Holy Spirit and with love this blessed child can teach the world about our Creator and about our King.

Let us see love in all things. Let us fear neither life nor death. Let us hope and trust in the Almighty God with all of our heart, with all of our soul, with all of our mind and with all of our strength. His Spirit lives and dwells within His chosen children. The children of God. The children of Israel. The children of Jesus Christ.

Father, cause us to do what is right, and what is just, and what is fair at all times.

There is no reason to hurry. There is no reason to doubt. God and Jesus rule the universe in righteousness.

The Holy Spirit is our friend. The Holy Spirit is God's invisible guide for us.

He is love exceeding light, water never ending and faithful despite our shortcomings.

We battle and war against the unseen, O yes, but my Father God is the God and Lord of the visible and the invisible!

Help those who are in need when you are able to. Help those who are in need when you are unable to.

God, Jesus and the Holy Ghost are faithful, true and dependable.

Although my Father sometimes waits to the last second to answer us, He owns and controls all of the seconds.

He is my Father. I am His child. In Him I trust and in Him I hope.

How can I not hope and trust in my Father? He gave me His Son and He gave me my son and my daughter.

In the name of the
Father, the Son and
the Holy Ghost

Amen and Amen
Copyright © 2008

The Joy of being a Child of Christ

A prayer of Mark Berryhill

Patience, kindness, love and gentleness. Concentrate on God's Word. Meditate on the Word of God.

Consider how wonderful it is to be alive. Consider how wonderful it is to be a child of Christ.

I know that He loves me. I know that I love Him. Try and prove our hearts my Lord and my King.

Consider how beautiful the universe actually is. Consider the power God exerts each day and yet for Him it is nothing for He is the Creator and sustainer of Heaven and earth.

The disobedient children are reserved for the day of wrath. The disobedient are reserved for the day of wrath.

Obey the Lord. Learn His commandments. Know the Word, live the Word and teach the Word my son and my daughter.

Graciousness, beauty and comfort are gifts from the Father of lights.

In the name of the
Father, the Son and
the Holy Ghost

Amen and Amen
Copyright © 2008

And then He Showed me the Cross

A prayer of Mark Berryhill

The question is often asked, "Why are we here?"

We are here to serve the Lord. We are here to learn, practice and spread the gospel of Jesus Christ.

Focus on the eternal. Focus your thoughts on the things which are good. Focus your total being on serving Jesus Christ.

Have you considered how much God, Jesus and the Holy Spirit love you? Consider and walk with Him holding your hand.

Except we have trials and tribulations, how could we appreciate the times of prosperity?

Consider. What is true prosperity? What is wealth? God's children. Your children and mine. Father, please help us to learn and obey Your Word.

Can you see the open pastures with beautiful grass and beautiful trees? Can you smell the soft falling rain? Can you see His strength lying within the strong gray and white clouds? God's strength is in His clouds.

Marriage is a gift. Intimacy is a gift. The child of God is the gift.

Keep the marriage bed pure and undefiled for the prostitute has slain many a strong man. Man without realizing has taken hold of death and hell by sharing His body with the prostitute.

Thank God for the gift of His child. Thank You, Father, for the blood of your Son that makes me whiter than snow.

Warn your friends! Walk in the light! Walk in obedience to the commandments of God!

Rivers of waters. Mountains, hills and rolling plains. All that God desires is obedient children.

Uprightness of heart. Uprightness of mind. Purity, undefiled in the flesh and in the Spirit.

Eternal verses the temporal.

Heaven is prepared. Are you prepared to spend eternity in Heaven, or will you spend eternity on fire?

Be wise to do good, not wise to do evil. Let us, let our yes be yes and our no be no.

There is a time to speak and a time to listen.

In God and with God, this young man can evangelize every nation under the Heaven.

I asked Jesus, "How much do You love each child?" He answered me. He showed me the cross.

In the name of the
Father, the Son and
the Holy Ghost

Amen and Amen
Copyright © 2008

In Christ there is Eternal Life

A song of Mark Berryhill

In Christ there is eternal life. In obedience to the Word of God is life eternal.

Certainly by His wonderful grace we are saved, but by our words and our works we will be judged.

What is love? What is life? What is important? What does God stand for?

God is love. God is life. Obedience to God's Word is important. God stands upright and will judge the world in righteousness.

We must walk according to His commandments, for each of us will give an account to Him for our actions.

Father, help us to walk perfectly before you all the days of our lives.

Lord Jesus, I know that You can do all things. I know that the breath of life is held by Your hand.

For I can say I have walked in the valley of the shadow of death with my Lord God and my Lord Jesus.

He sustained me. He loved me. He picked me up and he helped me to stand upright. Therefore, I will trust in the Lord all the days of my life.

We must teach our children the Word of God each day. We must help the Lord write His Word on their hearts and on their minds.

O Lord, our LORD, thank You for today. Thank You for the gift of life and eternal life.

Read Genesis One. Write down on a piece of paper how much wisdom God shows His children in chapter one of Genesis.

Heaven is real. Hell is real. Spend your time here on earth loving and diligently seeking the face of our King.

We will walk in the shadow of the Almighty for He has spread His powerful wings over our heads!

Lord God, thank You for Jesus. Jesus, thank You for loving each one of us. Help us and teach us to walk in the light.

In Jesus and with Jesus we can evangelize the world overnight. In God and with God we can light the world for the King of kings!

Listen to these words. Listen to these sayings. There is no wisdom nor knowledge but the wisdom and knowledge of God.

In the name of the
Father, the Son and
the Holy Ghost

Amen and Amen
Copyright © 2008

In the Womb of the Mother

A prayer of Mark Berryhill

Have you considered how precious and beautiful a new born baby is?

They are so delicate. Their little hands and little feet are so precious. I have wondered and considered how long do you suppose it took God to figure out how to form the beautiful child in the womb of the mother?

We too often take for granted our gifts from the Father of lights.

The cries and screams of the newborn are because he already craves for the love, care and nurture of both mother and father. The child. The newborn child. The young child. The child that loves the Lord will write his Father's book in his heart and in his mind.

God created us in His image and in His likeness. We are like Him. We laugh, we love, we are happy and we are sad. We care and we give because we love.

It is better to give than receive. There is one thing for certain, no two things for certain; man has no control over the day of his death. Man will spend eternity with the Lord or without the Lord.

O Lord my God, in You I trust. O Lord our God, in You will we hope.

I will hope in You, for I know that Your love for the child exceeds the light surpassing the Heavens!

Father, the children are Your great reward! You chose the greatest of the rewards!

God is my Father. Jesus is my Savior. I will lay down my life for them or for any child.

Let us learn to love beyond human comprehension. Let us have the faith to know that our name is written in the Lamb's Book of Life. By faith in Christ, by faith in our love for Him and by His faith that He has in His Father, we will evangelize every nation under the Heaven.

By His power and by His might we will conquer every nation under the Heaven in the name of the Father, the Son and the Holy Ghost.

There is no fear of death when you are a child of the King. There is no fear when God loves you as He does His own Son.

I consider. Certainly, Jesus is God's Son, but I know that they never leave any of their children.

God is life. God is light. God is love. In His Son there is eternal life.

How old are you today? How old were you yesterday? How old will you be tomorrow?

Will you be ready for your last day? Can we say we did our best for the Lord?

Lord Jesus, thank You for love, for life, for Your Word and for our children!

Each day brings forth a new beginning. Each morning You will hear my voice, my Lord and my God. At noontime You will hear a prayer of thanksgiving. At night, in the night watches, You will hear the voice of this child.

Seek the face of the King! Know and be certain that your every step is under the shadow of His wing.

Christ is King. He reigns. His work is to Shepherd and Bishop our souls.

When someone is hurting, what will you do? When someone needs love, what will you do? When someone hasn't any money, what will you do?

Will you take it with you on the day of your death?

Nothing belongs to you and nothing belongs to me. It is the Lord's; you and I are bought at the price of our King.

Glorify the Lord in both body and Spirit.

Father, thank You for having saved my life. I pray You will teach me and these children Your wonderful and magnificent Word.

In order to obtain, there must first be the goal. The goal is eternal life. God's Word, God's Son and God's Spirit are our guide.

Help us Father to be obedient to You. Help us, lead us and guide us in everything we do.

By faith, by love and with You, we can evangelize this little city. O Lord our Lord, how great and awesome are Your ways!

Father, thank You for my precious brother. Thank You for my precious sister. Father, thank You for our parents who fret over us as You fret over them.

Jesus, thank You for our children. Thank You for hearts of gold, hearts of silver and hearts of love.

In the name of the
Father, the Son and
the Holy Ghost

Amen and Amen
Copyright © 2008

Yahweh is His Name

A prayer of Mark Berryhill

His name is Yahweh. His name is Lord of lords and King of kings.

He rises early and instructs His children in His ways. They are attentive to His voice. They know the call of the Most High.

Know God. Love God. Trust Him with Your little ones. Know that He is with them at all times.

Know that He has commanded His angel to protect them for they are His.

Love God. Trust God. Know God and what He expects from you. Love Him more than you love yourself or life.

Gain knowledge. Gain understanding. To be able to learn. To be able to obey.

What does He demand? Why is He so demanding? He demands total loyalty to Him. He is so demanding because He loves you and wants to protect you temporally and eternally.

He is the judge. He is the final word of our eternity. Let us spend eternity with God. Walk in the light as He is in the light.

God, Jesus and the Holy Ghost. Blessed be the God of the armies of the angels of Heaven.

He stands tall. He stands perfect. He stands beside you because He loves you.

He is my Father, He is my Lord. He is my friend.

Love, life, laughter and joy. Happiness, gladness; all because of a little boy.

He wrote a book. He wrote a story. The story is His little boy.

O the love and wisdom God will reveal to mankind.
He wrote. He wrote a story. The story is His little boy.

In the name of the
Father, the Son and
the Holy Ghost

Amen and Amen
Copyright © 2008

The Light, the Invisible Friend

A song of Mark Berryhill

The invisible friend is the Holy Ghost.

He is your invisible friend as well as mine.

Who is He? Except He dwell within us, we would be as Sodom and Gomorrah.

He is our guide. He is the light of the world!

The Holy Ghost. The Holy Spirit of God. The Spirit of Jesus Christ.

Walk in accordance to His commandments. Walk with Him as He walks with us.

He never tires from His work; as is with wisdom, His joy is in leading the hearts of men in the pathway of righteousness.

Holy Spirit, Holy Ghost, Spirit of God, Spirit of God.

Love us and lead us to our eternal home. Please teach us the Word of God.

Teach us wisdom. Teach us knowledge. Give us love. Give us You!

And now we see there are three: the Father, the Son and the Holy Ghost.

In the name of the
Father, the Son and
the Holy Ghost

Amen and Amen
Copyright © 2008

Showers of Blessings

A song of Mark Berryhill

The light that exceeds the Heavens; who is the light that exceeds the Heavens?

Can you tell me His name? Can you tell me His Son's name?

Diligently seek God. Know that He is a rewarder of those who diligently seek Him.

Love, laughter, life and joy. The Holy Ghost is your friend and mine.

What is important? What do you desire? Eternal life is important. Eternal life with the Lord is now your desire.

Walk with Him. Talk with Him. He hears your every word. He knows your every thought.

He is good. He hates evil. He is love. He is life. He is the light of the world.

Friends and friendship. To give is better than to receive.

Kindness, gentleness, discipline, patience and charity.

Love reaching beyond all stars. Love that reaches beyond the Heavens. The love God has for His child and for you.

He is our Father. He is our friend. He has already given us far greater than we deserve.

Whisper gently to the one you love and tell Him that you love Him. He hears your every thought.

Walk with Him. Talk with Him. Love Him because He first loved you.

Love conquers all things. Love is the reason for you and me.

Showers of blessings. Showers of rivers of waters. Flowers of all kinds and of all colors. Beautiful to the eyes and to the smell.

He created everything beautiful. Walk with Him. Talk with Him. Live in the light and spend eternity with Him.

He loved you first. He created you. Love Him and thank Him for the showers of blessings.

In the name of the
Father, the Son and
the Holy Ghost

Amen and Amen

The God of our Daily Lives

A song of Mark Berryhill

How many nations are there on the earth? How many languages are spoken? Raise up laborers for the harvest, Lord of the harvest.

The fields are right for the harvest. Father, please teach the world Your Word. Place within us the desire for righteousness and holiness.

Place within the hearts and minds of our children Your great Word, my Lord, and my God.

Give us the Holy Spirit without measure. Help us to walk worthily of Your high calling.

We will walk in the Spirit. We will please our King. We will live and walk in the Spirit of the Lord.

Gray clouds, soft and so low, and yet I will not watch the clouds.

Father, Lord Jesus and Holy Spirit, help us to walk in Your light and in Your love.

O Lord, thank You for Your Son. O Lord, our Lord, walk with us and talk with us while we are young and tender, and when we are old and feeble.

It was a small house and it was a beautiful country setting, an elderly woman lived in the house.

She was kind and she was so happy. She was continually praising and thanking Lord Jesus.

Jesus, she would say, Jesus, yes, He is the way. He is the way, the truth and eternal life.

She had a small house. She had the blessings of many children. She was good to me. She was kind to me.

She prayed often and fervently, and I knew that God heard her prayers.

Within the hearts and within the minds of Your precious children may You write Your Word, my Lord, and my God.

In the clouds lies His great strength. He is strong. He is my strong tower and He can be yours also.

Father, we love You! Father, we need You in all that we do! Lead us, love us, live, and dwell with us in our daily lives!

I remember a lake, two creeks and two ponds. Oh to be young again, to be carefree, to live a life free of worry. And then I consider, I am young, I am carefree, and I almost live a life free of worry.

God laughs! I know that He laughs, and I know that He cries for we whom he loves.

Lead us in Your strength and in Your righteousness, my Lord, and my God.

On the last day. Will you go with Jesus on the last day? Walk with Him. Love Him.

He loves you!

In the name of the
Father, the Son and
the Holy Ghost

Amen and Amen
Copyright © 2008

Father, Son and Holy Ghost

A song of Mark Berryhill

There were young boys playing football and hide and seek. They were friends and they remain friends.

How can you have friends if you are not willing to be a friend?

To have friends you must give your heart. To be a friend you risk being hurt, but life without friends is meaningless.

Care and love. Be faithful when others may run. Be willing to lay down your life for the ones you love.

He is true. He is faithful. He is demanding. He is our King. He reigns over the universe by the power of His right hand.

To love, one must give his heart. To love, one must give her heart. Certainly there is risk involved in opening ones heart, but the rewards far outweigh the risk.

He is Creator. He is Son. He is Holy Ghost.

He is our Father, He is our Savior and He is our friend.

Let us keep the commandments of our Lord.

Share with and care for those who are unable. Provide for the ones you love.

In the name of the
Father, the Son and
the Holy Ghost

Amen and Amen
Copyright © 2008

Gentle Giggles of Darling Daughters and Precious Sons

A song of Mark Berryhill

Lord Jesus, how are You this day? Lord Jesus, thank You for today. LORD God, we love You and want for You to be our God.

Live a life in the Spirit. Live a life given to the King of kings. Live a life lived for others and not for oneself.

Love. Laugh. Give. Care. Build up. Give hope.

Cry. Love. Desire truth and holiness. Walk in truth and holiness.

Listen to the gentle giggle of your son. Listen to the soft giggle of your darling daughter.

Now you see why the King of kings never tires.

He is full of love, full of laughter, full of joy, full of kindness and gentleness, full of compassion and full of goodness.

Feed us with Your great Word, my Lord and my God.

My daughter, my precious daughter, write your Father's Word on the table of your heart.

My son, my precious son, write your Father's Word on the table of your heart.

Giggles and laughter, joyfulness and happiness, sons and daughters, blessings from the Father of lights.

He never tires. He never leaves. He is your Creator and He is your Savior.

We are Spirit and we are flesh. From dust we came and to dust we will return.

Purity, godliness, holiness and righteousness. Jesus Christ came to seek and save that which was lost.

He is the King. He is a great King. He is faithful and He is true.

He is love. He is life. He is light.

Children trust Him with total abandonment. Children love Him because He first loved you and created you.

Walk with Him. Talk with Him. Love Him for He loves you. He is faithful and He is true.

Lord Jesus, thank You for our children.

In the name of the
Father, the Son and
the Holy Ghost

Amen and Amen
Copyright © 2008

Love Him, for He Loves You

A prayer of Mark Berryhill

An open heart. A disciplined heart. A caring heart. A loving heart.

An open heart. A heart that conceals nothing. A heart that seeks truth.

He moved slowly. He was beautiful. The joy he brings into life.

To be able to learn. To be able to love. To be able to care. To be able to give your heart for the ones you love.

To care. To share. To love. To forgive. To heal. To be happy. To be faithful to God and to your loved ones.

To know love. To know that you are God's child. To know that He will never leave you.

He stands tall. He rises early each morning and instructs His loved ones.

The mountains are so peaceful. The beauty of God's creation is wonderful.

Walking, watching, learning, sharing and caring. Living.

Without love, life is meaningless. Without God, eternity is wrath and destruction. With God, eternity is more beautiful than the life we now have.

Trust in the eternal leadership of Jesus. Know Jesus. Love Him with all of your heart, with all of your soul, with all of your mind and with all of your strength.

Father, how great You are! Father, thank You for saving this blessed child's life.

Share love. Share the gospel of Jesus Christ.

Walk with Him every day in the light. Exert total and absolute control over mind and body.

Not as a means for salvation "for by grace are ye saved through faith; and that not of yourselves: it is the gift of God: Not of works, lest any man should boast."[19] But by our words and our works will we be justified or condemned.

Love. Laugh. Cry. Hope. Give. Be a friend.

Open your heart to the ones you love. Forgive. Love. Care and share.

Walk with the Lord every day. Know that His powerful presence is always abiding nearby.

Your body and my body are the temples of God; therefore glorify the Lord in both body and Spirit.

Birth, life, death. So as the sun rises and sets, so is God's faithfulness to His children Israel.

Fathom love. Fathom Christ's love for you. I have considered and have tried to calculate God's love for His children, it is impossible; His love for His children is immeasurable!

His love for His children can neither be weighed nor measured!

We are like Him. He made us in His image. He is holy. We are created in true holiness and true righteousness.

Fathom the mystery of the all knowing God. To know life. To see death. To see life.

We are Spirit. We are flesh. Walk in the Spirit and put away the uncleanness of the flesh.

Pure hearts. Hearts of love. Hearts of life. Hearts inclined toward caring and hearts inclined toward sharing.

A heart of gold. A heart of silver. A heart of love. A kind word. A gentle hello.

"Daddy," she boldly proclaims, "I love God."

"Daddy," the child says," I want to go to Heaven."

My son, my beautiful son, my daughter, my beautiful daughter, write the Word of God on the table of your hearts each day He gives you life.

Wealth and poverty, time and chance happen to each of us. Intelligence has nothing to do with what is viewed as wealth in the eyes of the world.

Wealth is to give of ones self for another. Wealth is to feed and care for the less fortunate.

Love is of God. Love is from God. Love God. Diligently seek Him,

---

[19] King James Version Ephesians 2:8-9

obey Him and know that He is a rewarder of those who diligently seek Him.

He only needed someone to listen and someone to care.

It is far better to build up rather than tear down, my Lord and my God.

Exalt the other person. Openly love the other person. Blindly give your heart for the other person.

God is love. God of forgiveness. God of wrath for the continual sinner.

Care. Share God's Word with your son and with your daughter.

Know that God will deliver you through every trial that you are taken through.

Love God. Seek the face of the King. Be willing to lay down your life for the ones you love.

Enjoy the joy of life. Enjoy the joy of marriage. Enjoy the joy of knowing your wife.

Know that God blesses husband and wife, provided they are under His guidelines.

Love your spouse. Love her the way Christ loves His church.

Be kind. Be gentle. May you each walk and talk with the Lord of hosts every day of your life.

God of love. God of tender mercies. God of enduring and unfailing love. God of destruction. God of fury and God of wrath.

God is holy; therefore, we will seek His holiness.

Love. Beauty. We too often take for granted the beauty of God's creation.

Love Him. Exalt Him. Glorify Him. He is your Father, He is your Savior, and He loves you.

He is always with me. He is always near. He loves me; therefore, I will love Him.

Obedience brings rewards, while disobedience brings punishment.

Although I didn't walk as I should have, my friend was there listening and taking care of His child way before I considered how much I was needed.

My Lord and my God, in You will I hope. I will exalt You and I will love You.

Lead us in the pathway of righteousness for Your great names sake.

Be quick to listen and slow to speak for anger rests in the bosom of the fool.

My Father, I love You! My Lord, I love You! Spirit, I love You!

Teach me Your Word and Your ways.

Live in the Spirit. Fix your eyes on Jesus. Focus on nothing but evangelizing every nation under the sun.

It will be done! It has been done!

Meditate on God's Word day and night. Walk with Him, talk with Him. Love Him for He loves You.

In the name of the
Father, the Son and
the Holy Ghost

Amen and Amen
Copyright © 2008

By Faith in the Blood of the Lamb

A song of Mark Berryhill

Listen to God's Word. Act on God's Word.

Time continues eternally. Time never ceases. Once conceived in the womb of the mother, time races onward.

Time can be a blessing, and time can be a curse. God created time. God was before time.

On the day of the Lord, the day of the resurrection of the just, those who have walked in the pathway of evil will spend eternity without God.

Listen before speaking. Listen before speaking. Listen before speaking.

Listen often. Speak seldom. Speak truth. Speak words of honesty.

In our patience we possess our souls. A kind word softly spoken brings comfort. Can you see gentle waves dancing against the seashore?

Breezes, the breezes bring such desired coolness. The breezes are fresh against one's face. Enjoy and listen to the beauty of life.

Listen carefully. Respond slowly and after much thought. Better yet, let us have God's Word written on the table of our heart and let it do the responding.

Silence, silence before the Lord. Listen, silence. Listen, silence before the Lord.

Listen to the giggles and laughter of a baby boy and a baby girl.

Life is worth living. Life is worth giving.

Hearing the giggles and laughter of my son and my daughter made my life worth living.

In joy I will trust in God. In sadness He will be my refuge and my strong tower.

He is holy. He is righteous. He is my Father, and He is my friend.

I know that sometimes I provoke Him, but it is only because I love Him.

He never leaves me. I believe He claimed me for His own before the creation of the universe.

He gave us faith in the blood of the Lamb, and by our great faith in the blood of Jesus Christ we are made whole.

Be buried with Him in baptism. Be raised with Him and walk with Him in the newness of life.

We are born into difficulties and we are born into trouble.

Lord Jesus, thank You for having given your life for me and each of us who love You and need You so much.

Listen, silence. Time is precious. Time is eternal. Please, may you and I ask God for guidance in the management of our time.

He loves. He laughs. He cries. He created us in His image and in the likeness of Him.

In the name of the
Father, the Son and
the Holy Ghost

Amen and Amen
Copyright © 2008

As the Children of Light

A song of Mark Berryhill

As the children of light we walk in obedience to the King of kings.

As the children of the light we are sons and daughters of the Most High.

As the children of the light we dwell and walk in the light of Christ.

Jesus, King of kings, Lord of lords, Prince of Peace, Lamb of God. Our love. Our life. Our light.

There was a mountain. It was beautiful. The view as the sun rose was overwhelming. I know that God was present. I know that He was with me. I was in trouble and He was healing me.

Father, thank You for healing this way ward child. Thank You for Your Son Jesus, and for Your Word.

The view was spectacular. Words are inadequate to describe the beauty of the rising sun this particular morning.

At that moment, at that instant, I remembered one of Jesus' many names: Sun of Righteousness.

The view was breathtaking as I looked at the rising sun. The brilliance of the sun that day was greater, far greater than the brilliance of a sun standing still for Joshua.

For I remember the prayer the Holy Spirit prayed on behalf of the children throughout the world.

God is light. God is love. God is life. In Him there is no darkness. He is a God who demands true holiness and true righteousness.

There was a beautiful creek and a beautiful pond. The water was gently and softly flowing through the small creek.

The water was crystal clear. The water was pure. The water was clean.

I pray Father, that You will never forsake Your children Israel.

Lord God, Lord Jesus, Holy Ghost. The Blessed Trinity. Father, Son and Holy Spirit.

The winning team. Walk in the light of our Lord.

God is a God of love. God is a God of compassion and tender mercies.

He is also a God that requires His children to walk in the light as the children of light.

I run. God runs with me. I walk and He walks beside me. I laugh and He laughs. We cry and He cries.

I believe that in all wisdom and in all knowledge God's heart is the heart of gold.

He created us. He died for us and He carries us.

To give is far better than to receive. To love is far better than to hate. To forgive is far better than to seek revenge.

Give me patience Lord God, and train us as warriors for Your holy kingdom.

He is the light. He is the life. He is the love.

His Word, His great Word, sustains the Heavens and the earth.

Jesus is His name. Jesus, Son of God, Son of man, Son of the Most High God.

In the name of the
Father, the Son and
the Holy Ghost

Amen and Amen
Copyright © 2008

Loving, Caring and as Trusting as the Child

A song of Mark Berryhill

Father, Lord Jesus, Holy Spirit, how are You doing today? There are so many beautiful children for You to carry.

I know that You have already placed them in Your bosom my Lord, my God.

"Daddy, Daddy," the young girl asks, "can you get me a princess dress?"

hearing that from my daughter made me realize how wonderful God's place must be. He has so many sons and so many daughters asking so many things.

Each morning He rises early and instructs His loved ones in His Word.

Father, I love You! You have become a challenge for me.

Lord Jesus, teach me Your Word. Teach me to live the remainder of my days in the Spirit and in perfection.

Not as a means of salvation, but because I love You and I fear You so.

The fear of the Lord is clean and pure. It is wonderful to fear and love the King of kings.

The Lord is our strength, the Lord is our hope, and the Lord is our strong tower.

The innocence of God's child. The beauty, the untold beauty of the child is His great reward.

They are so loving, so caring, and so trusting.

May we become as they are my Lord, my God.

Higher than the Heavens and farther than the east is to the west, is my Father's love for His children Israel.

Jesus Christ. The Messiah. The King. I AM THAT I AM. Prince of Peace. Holy One of God.

Your child and my child watch and hear everything we do and say. Be an example to them in all godliness and holiness.

In a word, with one word, I will describe my relationship with my Lord. I need You!

In the name of the
Father, the Son and
the Holy Ghost

Amen and Amen
Copyright © 2008

Father, We Need You and Jesus

A song of Mark Berryhill

As Solomon wrote, "Let us hear the conclusion of the whole matter: Fear God, and keep His commandments: for this is the whole duty of man."[20]

Let us look into our eyes and be able to know that in the depth of our soul we belong to the Lord.

There is no fear when one walks with the Almighty.

To be able to love, to be able to give, to be able to lift up rather than tear down.

My Father, to build up is much better than to tear down.

May I always exalt You and the other person and not myself.

We love. We live. We laugh. We have children who walk with God. We are happy. We are content.

Care for others. Share with others. Love God. Trust God. Obey God.

He is light. He is life. He is our love.

To learn the Word of God, we must allocate our time wisely. O Father, give us wisdom in the allocation of our time.

He was overlooking the river from the highest mountain. He was carrying his son in his right arm, holding him closely to his bosom.

The river of God was full. There was rejoicing. Happiness, laughter, kindness and love.

Know truth. Know Jesus. Love Him more than you love yourself.

May we give You our hearts, our Lord, our King.

Mold us. Hold us. Shape us into the image and likeness of Your Son, and our Savior, the Lord Jesus.

Father, help us to pursue the fruit of the Spirit. Give us love,

---

[20] King James Version Ecclesiastes 12:13

joy, peace, longsuffering, gentleness, goodness, faith, meekness and temperance.

A prayer to the God of Israel. A prayer to the King.

Father, we love You and we need You in all that we do.

In the name of the
Father, the Son and
the Holy Ghost

Amen and Amen
Copyright © 2008

He was Dancing

A song of Mark Berryhill

He was dancing. He was dancing. He was dancing and He was singing songs of joyfulness.

I could feel Him but I could not catch Him.

He was dancing. He was so happy and He was so full of joy. He was skipping. He was skipping through the hills and through the mountains.

I know that He walks beside me. I know that I am His. I know that He is mine.

He was skipping through the mountains. He was singing. He was so happy. He was joyful.

What is it Jesus? What is it? Lord Jesus, why are You so happy?

The children, they are all His.

He never tires. He is Spirit. He is faithful and He is true. He is love and He is light.

He is life. He is the breath of our life.

Oh to be loved by the King of kings. To be loved by the Most High.

He was dancing in the cool of the night. I could feel His presence; I know that it was Jesus, but I could not catch Him.

His love is enduring. His love is undying. His love is why He gave His life for you and me.

Joyfulness, happiness, life without struggles, and yet how could Jesus be our faithful High Priest without struggles?

When I felt Jesus dancing and singing, I began to sing and I wanted to dance.

At that moment I remembered how David loved, sang and praised God with all of his might because God had chosen him king.

Jesus was dancing. He was full of joy. He was skipping through the mountains as a little boy and yet, it was for all of the little boys and all of the little girls.

They are His. He is their God. He is the King. He is the Governor of His people Israel.

Sing, praise the Lord, sing, and see what wonderful and beautiful paintings you see.

He is full of love. He is full of compassion, tender mercies and truth.

His Father and my Father is JEHOVAH. God of all things.

In Christ there is hope. In Christ, there is love. In Christ and with Christ you can move mountains.

He loves you! He is your Creator and He is your Savior. Walk with Him. Talk with Him. He loves you and He will be your friend for eternity if you obey Him.

There is an eternal reward for obedience. There is an eternal penalty for disobedience.

As the story unfolds, we can see that God will never leave nor forsake His children Israel.

On You Lord Jesus, and on You Lord God, we depend.

Be attentive to the cries of Your children Israel.

I have often considered the beauty and innocence of the newborn child. And now Jesus says, Mark, have you considered the beauty of the elderly child?

He has walked with me and I have walked with him.

She has walked with me and I have walked with her.

He is willing to die for me.

She is willing to die for me.

I felt Him dancing. He was singing. I saw Him skipping through the mountains and through the hills.

He said, Mark, My child, have you considered the beauty of the elderly child?

He has walked with me and I have walked with him.

She has walked with me and I have walked with her.

I created him, He said. I created her, He said.

Do you think that I would not walk with them?

Oh the love and the wisdom God will reveal to mankind.

Son of God, Son of Man. Jesus reigns over the world by the power of His right hand.

He is white. She is white. He is yellow. She is yellow. He is red. She is red. He is black. She is black.

Jesus, Lord Jesus, please write Your Word on the hearts and minds of Your children Israel.

My son and my daughter, Jesus loves you so. Write His Word on the table of your hearts.

In the name of the
Father, the Son and
the Holy Ghost

Amen and Amen
Copyright © 2008

Three Burgundy Hearts

A song of Mark Berryhill

He is wise because He rises first. He rises early and instructs His saints in correct paths.

Listen to the cry of the hurting. Do you hear the unnecessary cry of the hurting?

Three hearts. There are three hearts of pure love. Three burgundy hearts weeping and pouring blood.

His name is Father, Son and Holy Ghost.

Train up the child in the daily admonition and nurture of the Lord.

Where is your heart? Is your heart on Christ? Is your hearts concern His hearts concern?

Within the Spirit of Jesus is where this young man desires for his children to reside.

Father, cover us with the blood of the Lamb.

Baptism into Jesus and walking in the light. It is a joy seeking the God of all things.

Hearts of love. Three hearts drawn as three hearts on valentine's day; but I see the pain and blood flowing freely from each heart. How great is the blood of God's Lamb?

He is risen and He is coming. Even so Lord, come quickly, Hallelujah.

In the name of the
Father, the Son and
the Holy Ghost

Amen and Amen
Copyright © 2008

They are as the Children

A prayer of Mark Berryhill

To understand time and judgment. To see in the invisible world of spirits.

To see and know how powerful the blood of the Lamb actually is.

Each of us will give an account to the Father, and our Lord Jesus for our actions.

Lord Jesus, help our actions and motives to be pure and to be to protect Your children.

To know love. To know Jesus. To love God. To seek Him with all of your heart, with all of your soul, with all of your strength.

They are as children. Father, Son and Holy Ghost. They are as the children.

Holy, absolutely but undoubtedly They are as the children.

They run, They walk, They fly, They laugh, They love and They cry.

Three hearts. Hearts shaped as valentines hearts. They are crying hearts.

Hearts showing indescribable pain. Three hearts pouring blood.

How great is the blood of the Lamb?

In the name of the
Father, the Son and
the Holy Ghost

Amen and Amen
Copyright © 2008

Falling Tears of an Orphaned Child

A prayer of Mark Berryhill

Charity, with Jesus, charity reigns. Overcome all struggles with charity.

With Jesus charity reigns. He is the wise one. He is the Holy One of God.

The Three for me are such a mystery.

Charity, with Jesus, charity reigns.

Let us love and care for the less fortunate. We are born to serve the sons and daughters of the Most High.

To rule for Christ we must be faithful servants. To govern with Jesus we must be faithful servants.

Servants of Christ. We are the Kings sons and daughters.

The father dies and the mother dies, but Jesus holds the little ones in His hand.

One God. One Son. One Spirit. Eternal One.

Exalt the Lord with me for He is good.

With Jesus charity reigns. With Jesus charity reigns. With Jesus charity reigns.

Father, Son and Holy Ghost. One and the same.

As you can see, we love the Blessed Trinity.

When walking with the Three, you can walk in love and in beauty.

If your heart becomes cold and hardened because of the cares of the world and the deceitfulness of riches, consider carefully what is truly important. The falling tears of an orphaned child. The precious tear of an orphaned child.

The child is the wealth. The child is the future.

To understand true love. To fathom the eternal victory that Jesus Christ won for His children at the cross.

To see the hurting. To see the children who are neglected and in need.

Father, help us to reach out and care for those who need Your love and guidance.

How do you heal the nation? How do you heal the people? He will heal the nations with His great Word!

What do you see? May I see the Lord Jesus before my face at all times.

Lord, cause your face to shine upon this holy ground.

Lord, cause your face to shine upon this holy ground.

Lord, cause your face to shine upon this holy ground.

What do you see? May we see the Lord Jesus before our faces at all times.

Father, thank You for the blood of the Lamb. The love the Lamb has for His children is indescribable.

The secret is in giving. Listen my children, my son, and my daughter, the secret is in giving.

In giving one receives blessings untold.

Lord Jesus, have we told You that we love You this day? Lord Jesus, have we told You that we need You this day?

My friends, my loved ones, exalt the Lord with me for He is good.

Goodness, what a joy it is walking in the power of the Holy Ghost!

Goodness, what joy it is walking with the King of kings holding your hand.

You see my children, what you thought you needed became irrelevant when the Father, the Son and the Holy Ghost envelope you with their majesty.

My son, and my daughter, Jesus loves you so. Remember His Words.

It is more blessed to give than receive.

In the name of the
Father, the Son and
the Holy Ghost

Amen and Amen
Copyright © 2008

May Charity Reign with Mankind

A prayer of Mark Berryhill

Father, how are You today? Father, have we told You that we love You this day?

Lord Jesus, how are You today? Lord Jesus, have we told You that we love You this day?

Holy Spirit, how are You today? Holy Spirit, have we told You we love You this day?

Pray, believe. Pray and believe and you shall receive.

Help the less fortunate. To be able to help the less fortunate is a blessing from God.

How do we help the less fortunate? How do we give them love, guidance and confidence?

Wise men, can you tell me how to give the orphaned child love, guidance and confidence?

Within the Father's book there is love, guidance and confidence.

Reach out to the needy. To understand the problem and to know the solution.

In a word the solution is known as THE WORD OF GOD!

We can give money and it is a temporal solution. Give them wisdom and knowledge, and they receive an eternal solution.

Wisdom dwelt with the Lord before the earth was. His delight is in leading and shaping the hearts of men and women.

With Jesus every one wins. He is King of kings and Lord of lords.

We have faith in His blood and walk in obedience to the Word. Lord Jesus, how are You this day my best friend?

When they were hurting did you help them? When they needed food did you feed them?

When the child cried did you cry with him? When the child cried did you cry with her?

May you see His face before you at all times. May you see beauty and holiness before you at all times.

May our children always see Your face before them my Lord, my God, my King.

What is life? What is death? What is the reason for existence?

My wise friends, can you tell me what life is? What is death? What is the reason for existence?

Life is Christ. Death in Christ is victory. The reason for existence is to serve the Creator of life and the giver of eternal victory.

You see wise men, you see wise friends, Jesus is the warrior.

As Solomon wrote, "She shall give to thine head an ornament of grace: a crown of glory shall she deliver to thee."[21]

I perceive that my God is a God of beauty. I perceive that our God is Creator of beauty.

Father, teach us Your Word. Write Your Word on the table of the hearts of these precious children.

Father, we pray for humility of heart and for obedience to the Word. Father, as charity reigns with Jesus, may it reign with mankind.

In the name of the
Father, the Son and
the Holy Ghost

Amen and Amen
Copyright © 2008

---

[21] King James Version Proverbs 4:9

The Secret: His Love for His Children

A prayer of Mark Berryhill

He is Lord and King. I will praise You Lord. I will pray unto the King of kings.

We look unto the Lord. We look and reach for the Most High God.

He is always there for you and for me. I asked Lord Jesus, Lord Jesus why are You always there for them and for me?

He responded by saying because I love them and I love you.

Seek the Lord with a pure heart. Let us love God with all our hearts, with all of our souls, with all of our minds, and with all of our strength.

The secret is His love for His children.

The wonderful fact about the God of Israel and the King of kings is that they are faithful and within them is truth.

In the name of the
Father, the Son and
the Holy Ghost

Amen and Amen
Copyright © 2008

Faith

A song of Mark Berryhill

Father, I pray for more faith. Study more He said, and more faith you will have.

Consider who the men and women of faith were and are.

They are those who study and meditate on God's Word relentlessly.

Father, we pray for faith. Study more He said, and more faith you will have.

"Faith comes by hearing, and hearing by the Word of God."[22]

Where does faith come from? Faith comes from the Father of faith. Faith comes from the Father of Israel.

Increase our faith O Lord we pray. He replies study more and more faith you will own.

"Faith comes by hearing, and hearing by the Word of God."[23]

Father, Father of faith, Father, Father of faith, in our hearts and minds place your great Word.

Father, Son and Holy Ghost, Father of faith, in our hearts and minds please write Your great Word.

Father, Son and Holy Ghost, our prayer is to have faith as the Blessed Trinity's faith. Faith, hope and charity.

Father, Son and Holy Ghost, our prayer is to have faith as the Blessed Trinity's faith. Faith, hope and charity.

Father, Son and Holy Ghost, our prayer is to have faith as the Blessed Trinity's faith. Faith, hope and charity.

In the name of the
Father, the Son and
the Holy Ghost

Amen and Amen
Copyright © 2008

---

[22] King James Version Romans 10:17
[23] King James Version Romans 10:17

The Eternal Power of the Blood of the Lamb

A song of Mark Berryhill

He wrote, "Let thine heart retain my Words, keep my commandments and live."[24]

Time is precious. Father, give us wisdom in what we study, and how we study.

Father, Son and Holy Ghost, how much wisdom can these precious children possess with You leading them?

Father, Son and Holy Ghost, how much wisdom can these precious children possess with You leading them?

The secret is in Christ's love for His children. The secret is in the eternal power of the blood of the Lamb.

Lord Jesus, thank You for the gift of time. Father, thank You for the gift of eternal life.

Father, Son and Holy Ghost, how much wisdom can these precious children possess with You leading them?

In the name of the
Father, the Son and
the Holy Ghost

Amen and Amen
Copyright © 2008

---

[24] King James Version Proverbs 4:4

A Prayer from a Child of the King

A prayer of Mark Berryhill

I can see Him and He is singing. His voice is as the voice of many waters.

I can see Him and He is singing. His voice is as the voice of many waters.

Father, Son and Holy Ghost, Oh, how I love You! You have become my hearts desire.

Father, teach us Your great Word. Lord Jesus, train us as You were trained.

"For though we walk in the flesh, we do not war after the flesh: For the weapons or our warfare are not carnal, but mighty through God to the pulling down of strongholds; casting down imaginations, and every high thing that exalteth itself against the knowledge of God, and bringing into captivity every thought to the obedience of Christ, and having in a readiness to revenge all disobedience when your obedience is fulfilled."[25]

He is the King of kings, Lord of lords and the bright and morning star.

He is true love. He is love that never abandons. God is the love that never abandons.

He is the light of men. He is the life of men.

Father, I love You! Jesus, I need You! Holy Spirit, dwell within the hearts of these precious children Israel.

In the name of the
Father, the Son and
the Holy Ghost

Amen and Amen
Copyright © 2008

---

[25] King James Version II Corinthians 10:3-6

As Jesus Embraces the Child

A prayer of Mark Berryhill

What do you see when you hear the name Lord Jesus?

What do you see when you hear the name Lord Jesus?

I see beauty, I see beauty. I see the smile, and hear the laughter of God's child.

What do you see when you hear the name Lord Jesus?

I see beauty, I see beauty. I see the smile, and hear the laughter of God's child.

I see beauty. I see beauty. I see the smile, and hear the laughter of God's child.

I see Jesus. I see Jesus. I see Jesus holding the child in His arms.

I see Jesus. I see Jesus. I see Jesus embracing the child.

You see my dear friend, in the name of Jesus there is beauty, happiness and love.

My dear friend what do you see when you hear the name Lord Jesus?

We see beauty. We see the smile, and hear the laughter of God's child.

May the children peacefully rest in the arms of our Lord.

In His strength the children do rest.

With His smile that reaches from west to east and with His voice that thunders and roars as the voice of many waters, He is King of kings and Lord of lords.

Can you see the rainbow that stretches from earth to the Heaven of heavens?

With beauty and with love this blessed child of the Most High will get all of these precious little lambs taught God's Word.

Gentle flowing rivers of waters, fields with green grass stretching endlessly.

Trees reaching from the earth to Heaven rest peacefully in the background.

There are horses, magnificent horses, horses of varied colors and sizes.

The first one is white. He is the unicorn. On the unicorn rides the conqueror.

The riders of the black, the red and the pale horses appear magnificent, but the rider of the unicorn is the conqueror.

Can you see the gentle flowing rivers of waters with endless fields of green grass?

Trees reaching from the earth to Heaven rest peacefully in the background.

There are some handsome young boys and beautiful girls looking for the Comforter.

In the midst of His children is where the Wonderful Counselor resides.

Jesus is teaching them in parables. The children are attentive to the words spoken by the King of kings.

From His mouth flow the words of eternal life.

He is Master. Within His mighty right hand is the very breath that you and I breathe.

Within His powerful hand He holds the key to death and hell.

He is rejoicing. He is weeping with joy.

He can see the power of the cross, and of the blood of the Lamb.

The children are attentive to His words. One handsome young boy has blonde hair. One of the precious little girls has beautiful sandy hair with tiny freckles.

The children know that Jesus is the teacher who will love them throughout eternity; years without end.

The children are attentive to His words. Why? He is all knowing and all powerful.

His smile reaches from the east to the west. His love for His chosen children reaches beyond the unseen walls of the universe.

In Him, there is life. In Him there is love, joy and peace.

With Him and in Him you can do all things.

He is risen. He is coming. Hallelujah, even so, come quickly Lord Jesus.

My children there is one walk in this life. The walk in this life is with Jesus in the light.

In the name of the
Father, the Son and
the Holy Ghost

Amen and Amen
Copyright © 2008

A Prayer to the Wonderful Counselor

A prayer of Mark Berryhill

Wonderful Counselor. Prince of Peace. Alpha and Omega.

Jesus, thank You for the rain today. Jesus, thank You for Your faithfulness to Your children.

Lord Jesus, we exalt You this day. Lord Jesus, we will love You this day and for days without end.

He remembers His love for His children. His love for His children never varies.

He said, I will never leave you My child. Before the creation of the world the child was with Him.

Before the foundation of the world, the child was with Him.

Can you see the rainbows stretching over the city? They are rainbows designed with perfection in mind.

Look at the soft falling rain dropping gently from the dark gray overshadowing cloud. Can you hear the gentleness of the soft falling rain on the roof of the cabin?

Lord Jesus, Nathan has memorized the names of the books of the Bible from Genesis through Song of Solomon.

Lord Jesus, Nathan has memorized the books of the Bible from Matthew through I Timothy.

Lord Jesus, Evan has memorized the names of the books of the Bible from Genesis through Song of Solomon and from Matthew through I Timothy.

In the name of the
Father, the Son and
the Holy Ghost

Amen and Amen
Copyright © 2008

The Beauty of the Rainbow

A prayer of Mark Berryhill

Lord Jesus, why do You love the child? Lord Jesus, why do You love the child?

He is a part of Me, He said. She is a part of Me, He said.

I see him from beginning to end. I see her from beginning to end.

In creation, in existence, and in power, my Father JEHOVAH chose blood as the means of redemption for His children.

For Me to have died for the children He creates and loves with all His heart was a gift for Me.

Lord Jesus, why do You love the child? Lord Jesus, why do You love the child?

He is a part of Me, He said. She is a part of Me, He said.

I Am great He said, but My Father is greater than I.

To see the face of Christ before us at all times is now our desire.

To have my children see Jesus before them at all times is now my desire,

The young man said that he wants a new life. The young lady said that she wants a new life.

Seek the face of Jesus. Seek the face of Jesus. Seek the face of Jesus.

Let us put away the sin that so easily hinders us from properly serving our Lord.

Pray, fast, and be holy for you are His son. Pray, fast, and be holy for you are His daughter.

Mark My son, I love these children. Mark, My son, I love these children.

When you see their hearts as the heart of My Father's, then I love these children with all of My heart.

He sustains the universe and He carries the breath of life.

You were formed out of the dust of the earth He said, and you will return to the dust of the earth.

Love Me and seek My face He said. You are My bride. Be holy and seek My face. Pray and fast.

Serve me with all of your heart, with all of your soul, with all of your strength.

Draw near unto the Lord and He will draw near unto you.

Exalt the Lord with me for He is good.

In the name of the
Father, the Son and
the Holy Ghost

Amen and Amen
Copyright © 2008

Pray, Study and Fast

A prayer of Mark Berryhill

Christ Jesus is life. Christ Jesus is the reason for existence.

He wants to be loved by each one of us. He owns us. He bought each one of us at the tree of Calvary.

Looking back to the cross is such a joy for me. The victory that Jesus won for mankind at the cross is overwhelming.

We were a lost people, and now we are a found people.

Serve the Lord with prayer and fasting.

Serve the Lord with diligent study. May Your Word become my heart and my children's heart my God, my King.

Obedience after baptism is a blessing from the Father of lights.

By His great power and strength we exist.

Order our steps my Lord, my King. He has a heart bigger than the world.

In all wisdom it is our Father who owns the heart that is bigger than the universe.

If you question Me in this statement, consider, would you allow for your only son to be crucified for sinners such as you and me?

Our Father is limited neither by time or love, for the Holy Ghost has an infinite supply of time and love.

Walk in the light. Do not sin. Seek out the things which please the Lord and do them.

Avoid evil and do good. Seek the Lord with all of your heart, with all of your soul, with all of your strength.

Each morning brings joy and happiness while serving Christ.

Evenings bring joy and happiness while serving Christ.

Father, open the doors so that we can study, pray and worship You all day every day.

May You be exalted every day and every moment of everyday.

Place Your name on our hearts and minds. Walk us in the light of Your Word.

Father, thank You for Jesus. Lord Jesus, thank You for Your blood. Holy Ghost, thank You for carrying each one of us.

Serve the Lord. Walk in the brightness of the King of kings.

Holy, holy, holy is the Lord God Almighty.

Resist the temptation of the flesh. Resist all evil.

Serve the Lord with prayer and fasting.

Study and meditate on God's Word day and night.

"For though we walk in the flesh, we do not war after the flesh; for the weapons of our warfare are not carnal, but mighty through God to the pulling down of strong holds; casting down imaginations and every high thing that exalted itself against the knowledge of God, and bringing into captivity every thought to the obedience of Christ; and having in a readiness to revenge all disobedience when your obedience is fulfilled."[26]

The time is at hand. Serve the Lord with me for He is good.

In the name of the
Father, the Son and
the Holy Ghost

Amen and Amen
Copyright © 2008

---

[26] King James Version II Corinthians 10:3-6

Inspired by Love

A prayer and a song of Mark Berryhill

The pain that He feels is indescribable. The pain that our Father feels, because of the rampant sin, cannot be expressed or written with words.

However, each morning light brings hope that another child will walk with Him.

You and I are His, He says. Walk in the light of My Son Jesus.

Study and meditate on His Word day and night.

Become as He is. Become as the Lord. He is all powerful. He is the Almighty.

There are too many tears flowing from the eyes of the Father. Set the world on fire for the King of kings.

Walk with the King in righteousness. Walk with the Lord in truth and in equity.

Lord Jesus, thank You for Your victory at the cross. Lord Jesus, help us to walk with You in truth and in equity.

Father, we love You! Jesus, we love You! Holy Ghost, we love You!

My son, do you believe that Jesus is the Son of the living God? I do he said, I now baptize you in the name of the Father, and of the Son and of the Holy Spirit.

My daughter, do you believe that Jesus is the Son of the living God? I do she said, I now baptize you in the name of the Father, and of the Son and of the Holy Spirit.

My precious child, my precious, precious child, you belong to the Lord.

My child, my precious, precious child, you now belong to the Lord.

In the tree there is a small nest. Within the nest is a small bird looking inquisitively as I pass by.

Let us not miss the beauty that God created for each one of us to enjoy.

Purity, holiness and love; three wonderful gifts from the Lord of life.

Have you ever considered the beauty of God's love for you?

His heart knows every beat of your heart. His heart, as we can see, is the heart of all good things.

Consider the beauty of the mountains. Consider the beauty of soaring eagles.

Consider the beauty of God's love for you.

Diligently seek the face of the Lord. Help Him write His Word in your heart.

Have you considered the beauty of the creation? Have you considered the beauty of the love between a Father and His Son?

Pray study and fast. Draw near unto the Lord and He will draw near unto you.

Father, forgive us of our sins. Help us to walk in the light while we journey here on earth.

Father, we exalt You this day! Father, we love You this day! Father, we need You this day!

Jesus, we exalt You this day! Jesus, we love You this day! Jesus, we need You this day!

Holy Ghost, we exalt You this day! Holy Ghost we love You this day! Holy Ghost we need You this day!

In the name of the
Father, the Son and
the Holy Ghost

Amen and Amen
Copyright © 2008

The Heart of God

By Mark Berryhill

Table of Contents

His Heart

A prayer of Mark Berryhill

His heart is full of love.
His heart is full of joy.
His heart is full of goodness; may yours also be.
The child is the reason for the creation.
His children will change the world with Him.
He can do all things, and so can you with Him.

In the name of the
Father, the Son and
the Holy Ghost

Amen and Amen
Copyright © 2008

A Soft Falling Tear

A prayer of Mark Berryhill

Do you see the tears that are flowing down the cheeks of your Father's face?

He has pleaded with you to study His word daily, why have you refused?

Tell me, my precious friend, why have you refused?

Do you see the tears that are flowing down the cheeks of your Father's face?

Consider the love a mother has for her newborn daughter. Have you ever considered the love a mother has for her newborn daughter?

Have you considered the love a father possesses for his son?

God's love for you is immeasurable.

Listen to His soft voice as He weeps, I love you with all that I AM!

Listen to His soft voice as He weeps, I love you with all that I AM!

In the name of the
Father, the Son and
the Holy Ghost

Amen and Amen
Copyright © 2008

A Reason to Love II

A prayer and a song of Mark Berryhill

The innocence of newborn children, and the love brought forth into our hearts because of their goodness, makes our very lives worth living.

Their precious little hands and feet are sculptured by the most brilliant artist ever known to the human race; His name is JEHOVAH.

Shout to the Lord with songs of praises because His mercy will endure forevermore.

In the name of the
Father, the Son and
the Holy Ghost

Amen and Amen
Copyright © 2008

The Goodness of Life

A prayer of Mark Berryhill

Life passes by as quickly as do the lightning bolts of Gods right finger as they dart through the rain filled sky.

Life is created by the Creator of life, and there is no other who deserves all of the praise, glory, honor and power as He does.

Life is created to be enjoyed, and with each breath You give us, may we praise You Almighty Father.

Life is good, enjoy the goodness and beauty created by the most brilliant Supreme Being there will ever be.

In the name of the
Father, the Son and
the Holy Ghost

Amen and Amen
Copyright © 2008

A Reason to Pray

A prayer of Mark Berryhill

Pray before you respond.

Pray a prayer of thanksgiving before you eat.

Pray prayers of thanksgiving unto our Creator for all of the beauty created by Him.

Pray a prayer of thanksgiving for the precious little boy brought forth unto you because of the Fathers great love for you.

Pray a prayer of thanksgiving for the precious little girl brought forth unto you because of the Fathers great love for you.

Pray a prayer of thanksgiving for the fervent prayers of parents who have gone on before us.

In the name of the
Father, the Son and
the Holy Ghost

Amen and Amen
Copyright © 2008

God of Hope

A song of Mark Berryhill

Hope must be the middle name of JEHOVAH.

Hope is given to each one of us because of the birth of a baby boy named JESUS.

Hope walks hand in hand with faith and love.

Hope rings forth throughout the Heavens because of the blood of the Son of the Great I AM!

In the name of the
Father, the Son and
the Holy Ghost

Amen and Amen
Copyright © 2008

His Great Rewards

A song of Mark Berryhill

Her thoughts are continually about God, and praises for Him from her lips melt His heart.

His thoughts are continually about God, and praises for God, from his lips, touch the heart of God.

She paints works of beauty in order to exalt her God, and the heart of God melts because of her great love for Him.

He writes words of beauty in order to exalt his God, and the heart of God is enlarged because of the brilliance of the words of beauty.

The sons and daughters of God are His great rewards.

In the name of the
Father, the Son and
the Holy Ghost

Amen and Amen
Copyright © 2008

265

His Faithful Love

A prayer of Mark Berryhill

God's love for you and His faithfulness unto you is as the soft falling rain which He caused to fall from Heaven this very day.

God's love for you will never be withdrawn from you because of His great faithfulness.

God's love for you and faithfulness unto you is as the painting of a garden of beautifully and delicately arranged flowers after a soft falling rain.

God's love for you is best demonstrated by the painting of a precious and innocent young man hanging on a cross with blood flowing from the crown of thorns placed within His head, and the stakes which were placed within His hands.

In the name of the
Father, the Son and
the Holy Ghost

Amen and Amen
Copyright © 2008

The Love of His Son

A song of Mark Berryhill

Holy Father, one soft falling tear has become a racing river of tears for a beautiful young maiden.

Holy Father, the war between good and evil will intensify, cause the blood of Your Son to shout forth and claim victory over evil.

Life in Christ is victory, while life apart from Christ is eternal separation from God.

Holy Father, let the soft falling tears of the beautiful young maiden be turned into tears of joy because of the words of beauty that you will write through her.

Holy Father, tell her that she is clothed in a dress of pure white because of the love of Your Son.

In the name of the
Father, the Son and
the Holy Ghost

Amen and Amen
Copyright © 2008

Heart of Joy

A prayer of Mark Berryhill

He came to earth from Heaven to save His children.

His middle name is unselfish.

His immense love for you surpasses even the distance that it is from the farthest star of the north to the farthest star of the south.

His very reason for existence is to love you.

His heart leaps for joy each time He hears the prayers of His called-out children.

His love and faithfulness are our strength and refuge!

He is the Great I AM!

In the name of the
Father, the Son and
the Holy Ghost

Amen and Amen
Copyright © 2008

All for JESUS

A song of Mark Berryhill

What we teach our children today is what our children will know tomorrow.

Father, pour your wisdom upon us, and teach us how to raise these precious lambs for You with Your leading.

Lord Jesus, thank You for the beauty of Your creation and for the gift and beauty of our precious children.

Holy Ghost, reign over our hearts and over the hearts of our children.

In the name of the
Father, the Son and
the Holy Ghost

Amen and Amen
Copyright © 2008

His Daughter

A prayer of Mark Berryhill

He is faithful. He is true.

He is just.

His smile shines radiantly from the farthest star of the west, even unto the farthest star of the east.

He desires peace, but He is prepared for war.

He is love and compassion.

He created the beauty of life.

In His right hand the very breath of our lives is held.

He brings goodness and joy into our lives.

She loves birds, cats and dogs. She is a daughter of the Most High. She is a princess.

In the name of the
Father, the Son and
the Holy Ghost

Amen and Amen
Copyright © 2008

An Infinite Love

A prayer of Mark Berryhill

Work is good, when our work is the work our LORD has called us to complete.

Never underestimate the importance of accepting Christ as your personal Savior, and walking with Him in His light thereafter.

Give your heart to our LORD, and love Him the way He loves you.

It was His love for you that placed Him on His cross.

The American Bald Eagle soars on the wings of the angels of the Everlasting Father.

In the name of the
Father, the Son and
the Holy Ghost

Amen and Amen
Copyright © 2008

The Beauty of Life

A prayer of Mark Berryhill

If you abandon a friend in their time of difficulty, were you a true friend?

If you abandon a friend when the storms of trial and tribulation attempt to destroy that friend, are you worthy to be called faithful?

Have you done today what Christ has commissioned you to do today? Have you helped to write His Word on the hearts of the children of this nation today?

Have you considered the beauty of the laughter of His precious children throughout the world today?

In the name of the
Father, the Son and
the Holy Ghost

Amen and Amen
Copyright © 2008

Sing and Dance

A song of Mark Berryhill

Holy Father, teach us to discern good and evil, even as You do.

Holy Father, cause Your children to do what is right in Your sight, not what is right in the sight of the world.

Holy Father, anoint us with Your love.

Holy Father, sing and dance with joy in Your heart over Your children, this very night!

Holy Father, we love You, and we need You and Your Word in our daily lives.

In the name of the
Father, the Son and
the Holy Ghost

Amen and Amen
Copyright © 2008

Sing unto the Lord

A song of Mark Berryhill

God is love, and in His right hand the breath of our lives is held.

God is life, and the blood of His Son Jesus Christ cleanses us from all sin and unrighteousness.

God is light, and in Him no darkness can be found.

God is holy, and so are we because of the blood of His innocent Lamb.

God is great, and no other can be likened unto JEHOVAH.

The precious children that He has entrusted unto us need His Word in their daily lives.

In the name of the
Father, the Son and
the Holy Ghost

Amen and Amen
Copyright © 2008

The Victorious Blood of Christ

A song of Mark Berryhill

Do you want to be closer to God?

Give your heart to Him, and serve Him with every fiber of your being.

Do you want to understand how much God loves you?

Ask Him for a child, and then you will begin to comprehend a Father's love for His child.

Do you want a strong marriage?

Obey Gods ordained order and the principals found within the Holy Scriptures.

Do you want the guarantee of eternal life?

Love God with all of your heart, soul, mind and strength, and know that you are saved!

God is faithful!

In the name of the
Father, the Son and
the Holy Ghost

Amen and Amen
Copyright © 2008

Love, Grace and Humility

A song of Mark Berryhill

The joy a mother experiences as her newborn baby girl is placed into her arms for the first time, must be a joy surpassed by no other.

The love a father experiences as he wraps his arms around his newborn son for the first time causes the new dad to know the love God possesses for each one of us.

I believe that love, grace and humility are the showers of blessings the precious children of this nation are destined to inherit from the Almighty.

The change of season covers us with fresh cool breezes and although Gods seasons change, His faithfulness and salvation belongs to you forevermore because of His immeasurable love for you.

In the name of the
Father, the Son and
the Holy Ghost

Amen and Amen
Copyright © 2008

A Ray of Light

A song of Mark Berryhill

Laughter is one of God's greatest gifts to His children.

Laughter turns difficult days into days of goodness.

Laughter brings the hearts of the children of God good health, and is as the fragrance of a beautiful rose.

Laughter is good and I thank God for people who know how to love and to laugh.

In the name of the
Father, the Son and
the Holy Ghost

Amen and Amen
Copyright © 2008

A Story of Love

A prayer of Mark Berryhill

Self-discipline creates rewards worth more than silver or gold, while lack thereof issues forth death.

Love, and the quality thereof, keeps one healthy, and she keeps no record of wrongs against others.

Peace rests upon the children of God who have fully placed there faith in Him.

Gentleness by no means constitutes weakness; on the contrary, she promotes strength and control.

In the name of the
Father, the Son and
the Holy Ghost

Amen and Amen
Copyright © 2008

Eye of the Storm

A song of Mark Berryhill

America, My beautiful America, why have you forsaken the straight path laid out before you by My servants the prophets?

America, My beautiful America, is not wisdom more valuable than gold, and understanding more precious than silver?

America, My beautiful America, where is the majestic banner that exalts the Father, Son and Holy Ghost?

America, My beautiful America, your heart has become hardened, and your ears are waxed shut, and yet, I love you with all that I AM!

America, My beautiful America, within the Holy Scriptures, the beauty of life is proclaimed.

In the name of the
Father, the Son and
the Holy Ghost

Amen and Amen
Copyright © 2008

Breath of Life

A song of Mark Berryhill

Father, we thank You for the gift of life.

Father, we pray that You will walk us in the pathway of obedience, and teach us to denounce disobedience.

Father, we pray that You will teach us how to love, and to never hate.

Father, we are so thankful for our beloved children, and we pray fervently for You to incline their hearts unto You.

Father, may You and You alone, be our children's great reward.

Father, thank You for mothers who love their children with all their hearts.

Father, thank You for fathers that love their children with all their hearts.

In the name of the
Father, the Son and
the Holy Ghost

Amen and Amen
Copyright © 2008

The Faithfulness of Christ

A song of Mark Berryhill

Precious friend, have you considered that the proper use of time is critical for the furtherance of the kingdom of God?

Precious friend, have you considered the beauty of the season, as she changes from warm weather unto a crispy and cool climate.

Precious friend, have you considered the amount of love Jesus Christ displayed for His children at His cross?

Precious friend, have you considered the good that God has brought forth today because of His immense love for us?

In the name of the
Father, the Son and
the Holy Ghost

Amen and Amen
Copyright © 2008

A Brilliant Light

A song of Mark Berryhill

Immanuel spoke; some listened and obeyed His words, while others refused the wisdom of God.

Immanuel translated means God with us, and there is no other name under Heaven whereby man can be saved.

Immanuel is the way, the truth and the life and the precious child held by your arms is because of His immense love for you.

Immanuel, place within the heart of Magdalena a love for these children that is as Your love for them.

Immanuel, thank You for the beauty of the sunrise, for the brilliance of the sunset, and for the perfection with which You created today!

In the name of the
Father, the Son and
the Holy Ghost

Amen and Amen
Copyright © 2008

Live for Christ

A song of Mark Berryhill

God has been faithful to you; will you be faithful to Him?

God loves you with every fiber of His existence; do you love Him in the like manner?

God sent Jesus to die for your sins, would you allow your son to be slaughtered for the sins of the world?

God softly whispers to me, My precious child, tell them that I love them with all that I AM!

In the name of the
Father, the Son and
the Holy Ghost

Amen and Amen
Copyright © 2008

JEHOVAH is Great

A song of Mark Berryhill

JEHOVAH reigns over Heaven and earth, and no one can be likened unto Him!

JEHOVAH is great, and nothing can hinder His ordained plans for the lives of our children!

JEHOVAH has all of the power, and His ownership of hell is the confirming sign!

JEHOVAH loves you with all of His being; give your heart to Him, and serve Him every moment of every day!

In the name of the
Father, the Son and
the Holy Ghost

Amen and Amen
Copyright © 2008

Heart of God

A song of Mark Berryhill

Love is from God, and He is faithful!

Joy is a gift from God, and He desires to rule over your heart!

Peace and holiness walk hand in hand, even as a newly married couple!

Longsuffering is as love, and keeps no record of wrongs!

Gentleness does not constitute weakness; on the contrary, she breeds strength!

Goodness is brought forth by a heart that truly cares!

Faith in Christ, and in His power, is how we will overcome the world!

Meekness and humility are as a brother and sister who never abandon!

Temperance, and the importance thereof, can save your life and your soul!

In the name of the
Father, the Son and
the Holy Ghost

Amen and Amen
Copyright © 2008

God is Love

A song of Mark Berryhill

Can you imagine the greatness of JEHOVAH?

Can you fathom the immeasurable love that resides within His heart for you?

Can you comprehend His power, or the infinite mercy that He extended to you at the cross of His Son Jesus?

Can you either measure or weigh the brilliance of JEHOVAH?

Can you name the stars by name each night as He does?

In the name of the
Father, the Son and
the Holy Ghost

Amen and Amen
Copyright © 2008

Love, Life and Laughter

A prayer of Mark Berryhill

Jesus Christ, bless the works of our hands, and the work of our children's hands.

Jesus Christ, let Your smile be seen from the farthest star of the west unto the farthest star of the east.

Jesus Christ, let Your love be manifested from sea to shining sea!

Jesus Christ, thank You for love, life and laughter!

Jesus Christ, thank You for wives that love You with every fiber of their being!

In the name of the
Father, the Son and
the Holy Ghost

Amen and Amen
Copyright © 2008

The Beauty of His Love II

A prayer of Mark Berryhill

Within the heart of God there is only love, and hate is no where to be found.

Within the heart of God there is a longing for His children to obey His voice, and to denounce the sins of the world.

Within the heart of God, faith and hope are as a faithful father and mother, while love is as the precious child born unto them.

In the name of the
Father, the Son and
the Holy Ghost

Amen and Amen
Copyright © 2008

An Evangelist Clothed in a Black Suit

A prayer of Mark Berryhill

The preacher boldly proclaims his undying faith in Jesus Christ, and states that those who accept Jesus as their personal Savior are indeed saved.

The preacher boldly proclaims that our lives are created by God to serve Him, for this is the very reason for our existence.

The preacher boldly proclaims to resist dating anyone outside the church, only marry a mate that is within the church,

The preacher boldly proclaims his love for the Holy Ghost, and knows with all confidence that the Holy Ghost can do all things!

In the name of the
Father, the Son and
the Holy Ghost

Amen and Amen
Copyright © 2008

A Reason to Smile

A song of Mark Berryhill

Life is wonderful, and the life to come will be even better.

Love is the greatest gift given to the human race, and can best be translated by the name Jesus Christ. Wisdom is worth more than gold or silver, and if one continues to apply her, she will bring the greatest rewards.

If you have lost hope, remember that the only reason we are here on earth is to tell the world about Jesus and to live for Him.

Life is not meaningless, on the contrary, she is a gift from the Creator of life, and she is to be savored.

Life, and Eternal Life are gifts from the Eternal One, and His name is Jesus Christ.

In the name of the
Father, the Son and
the Holy Ghost

Amen and Amen
Copyright © 2008

Love, Life and Light

A prayer of Mark Berryhill

God seeks peace and joy for His beloved, while hate seeks the death and destruction of the beloved of God.

Love desires to hear the beauty of the laughter of a young child, while hate ignores the cries of the precious hurting children of God.

Love is faithful and keeps no record of wrongs, while hate is never content or satisfied with the gifts offered from the Father of lights.

Love is the keeping of the commandments of God, and the enemy will do everything he can to keep you and your children out of the Word of God.

Love is greater than wisdom, and love is to be more valued than silver for nothing can be compared unto true love.

God is love.

In the name of the
Father, the Son and
the Holy Ghost

Amen and Amen
Copyright © 2008

A Song About Discipline

A song of Mark Berryhill

Discipline brings forth great rewards, and to love each other with all of our heart, soul, mind and strength requires a great amount of discipline.

Will you and I truly obey the lead of the Holy Spirit today, or pretend as if we did not hear His gentle voice?

Has the Holy Spirit told you and I what to do today, even years ago?

How much time will you and I invest in the Word of God today?

Bright futures are presented by a faithful King and His name is IMMANUEL!

Remember my precious friends that our lives are as a vapor and a mist when compared to eternity!

Father, let the face of Your precious Son be ever presently placed before our spiritual eyes.

Father, fill us with Your Word, and with Your wonderful Holy Spirit!

In the name of the
Father, the Son and
the Holy Ghost

Amen and Amen
Copyright © 2008

Omega

A song of Mark Berryhill

How much time will the children of God spend in His Word while in public schools of America today?

The most important thing our children can be doing today is to be studying the Word of God.

God recently placed a lonely cloud in a beautiful dark blue sky.

The cloud was painted by the fingers of the Almighty with exquisite precision and beauty, and the translation of the design of the cloud explains our Fathers faithfulness to warn a world that no longer seeks Him daily as instructed in the Holy Scriptures.

When society tells you that education and the pursuit of her is more important than the diligent daily study of the Word of God, tell the educators that the educators of Noah's day said the same thing and they all perished.

How soon will history repeat itself?

Will America repent and seek God daily, or will she scoff at God's warning and receive the punishment due unto her?

The open vision was a cloud which was formed in the shape of what is known in the Greek alphabet letter as Omega!

In the name of the
Father, the Son and
the Holy Ghost

Amen and Amen
Copyright © 2008

Jesus Christ Reigns

A song of Mark Berryhill

In life there are obstacles and difficulties and yet when our eyes stay focused on Christ He removes the obstacles that seem so overwhelming.

Jesus loves you with all of His heart!

Jesus will sing songs of beauty over you this very night because of His immense love for you!

Jesus longs for you to be filled with His Word and with His Spirit!

Jesus is love and He is not in the forsaking business!

Jesus is great and no other can be likened unto Him!

Jesus we love You, we need You and we thank You for the victory of Your cross!

In the name of the
Father, the Son and
the Holy Ghost

Amen and Amen
Copyright © 2008

Heart of Gold

A prayer of Mark Berryhill

Love is from God and God never fails!

Love persists when all other qualities have given up.

Love never forsakes, nor abandons.

Love is why God created the universe, and love is why He created you.

Love supersedes all other qualities, and our Father, is love.

Love causes parents to trust in our Father's wisdom and not our own.

Love is what a father and mother experience when a precious newborn baby is brought forth into the world.

Love is what a father and mother experience when they know the child is saved because of the Father's faithfulness!

God is love!

In the name of the
Father, the Son and
the Holy Ghost

Amen and Amen
Copyright © 2008

Blessed of God

A song of Mark Berryhill

Holy Father, cause Your mercy to rain down upon us.
Holy Father, cause Your love to rain down upon us.
Holy Father, cause Your goodness to rain down upon us.
Holy Father, cause Your greatness to rain down upon us.
Holy Father, cause Your compassion to rain down upon us.
Holy Father, cause Your faithfulness to rain down upon us.
Holy Father, cause Your glory to rain down upon us.
Holy Father, cause Your joy to rain down upon us.
Holy Father, cause Your truth to rain down upon us.
Holy Father, cause Your majesty to rain down upon us.
Holy Father, cause Your wisdom to rain down upon us.
Holy Father, cause Your knowledge to rain down upon us.

In the name of the
Father, the Son and
the Holy Ghost

Amen and Amen
Copyright © 2008

The Beauty of Life II

A prayer of Mark Berryhill

Life is for living, and life is for giving to the less fortunate.

Life is to be savored, and she is to be lived walking in the light of Jesus Christ.

Life may seem to present difficulties, but with our eyes on Christ, those very same difficulties become hidden opportunities.

Life, and living life to the fullest, is an art; as we learn to walk holding the hand of Jesus.

Life is beautiful, and learning to love Jesus with all of our heart, soul, mind and strength is a joy likened by no other.

God is the Creator of life, and because of His great victory, known as the Cross of Calvary; we are saved to the uttermost!

The blood of Jesus Christ and the power of His blood reaches from everlasting to everlasting.

The precious children are our Father's great rewards, and neither God nor His Son Jesus Christ will ever forsake them.

God will write His Word onto the hearts and minds of His beloved children.

In the name of the
Father, the Son and
the Holy Ghost

Amen and Amen
Copyright © 2008

Jesus Christ is Life

A prayer of Mark Berryhill

Jesus came to the earth to die for you because He loves you with all of His heart, soul, mind and strength!

Jesus causes the seeming lifeless trees to come to life once again as they begin to sing and dance because they are clothed with such beautiful leaves.

Jesus forms these precious and beautiful children in the wombs of their mothers, and it is our duty to raise them in His Word every day.

Jesus loves us because we are His creation.

Jesus causes the sun to rise and set each day.

Jesus names the stars by name each night as He sings.

Jesus spoke and created light.

Jesus can do all things, and so can you as He becomes your best friend!

Walk us in the light of Your Son Jesus Christ, Almighty Father.

In the name of the
Father, the Son and
the Holy Ghost

Amen and Amen
Copyright © 2008